HOW TO INTERVIEW

HOW TO INTERVIEW
The art of the media interview

Paul McLaughlin

Self-Counsel Press
(a division of)
International Self-Counsel Press Ltd.
Canada   U.S.A.

Printed in Canada

First edition: May, 1986
Second edition: January, 1990; Reprinted: February, 1992

Canadian Cataloguing in Publication Data

McLaughlin, Paul, 1950-
    How to interview

    Previously published as: Asking questions.
    (Self-counsel series)
    ISBN 0-88908-872-1

    1. Interviewing in journalism.   2. Interviewing in
radio.   3. Interviewing in television.   4. Interviews.
I. Title.   II. Title: Asking questions.   III. Series.
PN4784.I6M24   1990   070.4'3   C89-091633-0

Cover photo by Sherpitel/Image Finders, Vancouver

Self-Counsel Press
(a division of)
International Self-Counsel Press Ltd.
Head and Editorial Office
1481 Charlotte Road
North Vancouver, British Columbia V7J 1H1

U.S. Address
1704 N. State Street
Bellingham, Washington 98225

To my parents, for their courage and foresight in coming to Canada.

CONTENTS

ACKNOWLEDGMENTS

My thanks are due to the following people:

To Hilary McLaughlin, my sister and friend, for her diligent and perceptive editing of the rough manuscript; to Patricia Robertson, senior editor of International Self-Counsel Press Ltd., for her endless patience and expert editing; and to Kim Levis, for her research, interviews, hard work, and enthusiastic help in so many ways.

To Ann Fielding, Lynn Snelling, Anna Kohn, and John T. D. Keyes, for their valuable and greatly appreciated contributions; and to the approximately 100 interviewees, who gave their time and shared their ideas on interviewing with such generosity.

And to Xenia Splawinski, for her insightful analysis of the text, and loving friendship.

INTRODUCTION

This book is a personal interpretation of the interview process. It is not a textbook. The media interview cannot be reduced to a set of rigid rules and formulas. Although there are many methods or strategies that have proven successful in certain situations, each interview is a unique and special experience, and each interviewer has his or her own way of approaching it.

The subject of interviewing is a stimulating and complex one that has fascinated me since the day in June, 1973, when I picked up a telephone and did my first interview as a researcher for CBC Radio. Lacking any journalism education or experience, I was totally unprepared for what lay ahead. Talking to people had never been a problem for me, so I presumed that interviewing was no more than just chatting away until the conversation came to a natural close. I learned quickly (and painfully) that it involved far more than just blindly casting out questions and reeling in the answers.

What I soon discovered, and have continued to discover over the years, is that interviewing is an art form: an intricate discipline that combines preparation and spontaneity in a potent and sometimes dangerous mix. Like any art form, it's practiced on many different levels, depending on the innate talent, hard work, and creativity of its performers. At its best, what really takes place is an "inter-view" — a mutual process of looking inward (*inter* means "between"). The success depends on first understanding your own internal views. And the more self-awareness you cultivate, the greater the ease and skill you'll bring to the interview process. The word *interview* is derived from the French *entrevue/entrevoir*, meaning "to see *one another*," which is an important distinction not usually associated with its English counterpart. Herein lies the key to one of the most overlooked benefits of interviewing: the tremendous opportunity available to find out about yourself through discovering other people, their ideas, and your responses to them.

I've also learned that an interview is not simulated reality; it is not a game or job that doesn't count beyond the exercise of filling space or time and the requirements of meeting deadlines. On the contrary, an interview is very real, even in its most mundane or seemingly artificial moments. Whenever people communicate, a real interaction takes place. If you interview a parent whose child has just been murdered, the emotions you feel — guilt about questioning the parent at such a private time, fear of not knowing what to say, anger about the tragic event that has occurred — will have a profound effect upon you, even if that effect is just the blocking of your feelings. The parent's response, which could be anything from rage at the intrusion to the welcoming of a sympathetic ear, will also affect you. While this is an extreme example, variations occur with every interview. If you ask a stupid question, or don't know your facts, you'll feel embarrassed regardless of the subject matter or the importance of the guest. The degree may vary, depending on the circumstances, but the sensation will be all too real.

I raise this point because I think it's easy to slide into a way of thinking about interviews that glosses over reality. By looking at it primarily as a game, it makes it easier to cope with some of the less pleasant aspects of the task. For example, raking a businessperson over the coals in public (which is rarely enjoyable, even if you think the person deserves rough treatment) is not as hard to deal with if you consider all businesspeople to be crooks and therefore fair game for attack. Likewise, it's easier to see the interview as little more than entertainment, with the attack being an essential part of the show, no matter what it might do to the businessperson or his or her business. That doesn't mean you don't give people a hard time. What it does mean is that, before choosing your course of action, you stop and consider each interview as a real and unique event that will have definite consequences for you and your guest.

If you decide on your approach beforehand, much of the fear associated with interviewing is relieved. And interviewing can invoke a great deal of fear — fear of saying the wrong thing or of not knowing what to say; making a fool of yourself (sometimes publicly); hurting or embarrassing someone, particularly when dealing with sensitive subjects or with people under emotional stress; having to confront subjects that make you uncomfortable; not being tough enough or not living up to the stereotype of the detached, cynical journalist; being lied to, manipulated, or exploited without knowing how to recognize or combat it; incurring the wrath, hatred, contempt, or ridicule of the guest; being intimidated, threatened, or otherwise abused; and not being liked but needing to be liked.

But if you approach an interview well-prepared, and with a thoughtful understanding of why you're doing it, the confidence and clarity that results will help greatly to reduce your fears. The more you study the multiple dimensions of interviewing, and the more information you acquire, the easier it is to ask the right questions, tough or sympathetic, without fear.

When I speak of fear, I am not talking about the healthy tension that occurs in a successful interview. The excitement, unpredictability, and dangers that accompany interviewing generate tension and energy, which are necessary and healthy. Without some stress, the dynamic required for a successful interview would be diminished.

Interviewing has given me great pleasure for many years. I consider it a privilege to be able to ask questions of people and learn more about them and me. In the course of researching this book, I conducted over 100 interviews either in person or by phone. One or two, conducted with journalists now living in England, were obtained by sending questions and a cassette tape in the mail. Most interviews were arranged by phone; in a few instances I wrote letters and followed up with a phone call. The response rate was excellent, with only a small percentage declining to participate.

Although it was not possible to quote everyone I interviewed, the information provided was invaluable in helping me formulate the ideas presented. The conclusions I've reached, although influenced by many of the people I spoke with, are first and foremost my own, and quite a few have evolved in the year and a half it has taken to complete the book.

1
THE ART OF LISTENING

If I could write only one chapter about interviewing, it would be about listening. And if I could write only one sentence, it would be this. The more deeply you listen, the more eloquently people will speak.

Active, concentrated listening does not benefit only you, the listener. It also helps the speaker. Just as an actor playing Hamlet would have great difficulty delivering a soliloquy with feeling if the audience were distracted, an interviewer who does not pay complete attention to what a guest is saying will diminish the interviewee's ability to speak and the quality of what he or she says.

a. WHAT MAKES A GOOD LISTENER?

The key to being a good listener is to want to listen, which can require willpower and discipline. Unfortunately, few people are willing to make that effort. "Basically, listening for most of us is waiting for a chance to start talking again," says Stuart McLean, a radio documentary maker and the Director of Broadcast Journalism at Ryerson Polytechnical Institute in Toronto. "If you listen to two people talking, what you find is that the person who interjects is not listening. Instead of a conversation, you have two parallel, distinct narratives going on, one interrupting the other. I catch myself doing it — we all do it. Even when we are being what we think is sensitive — we're listening to some guy tell about how his wife has left him — the listener 'listens' by telling about when *his* girlfriend left *him*. We all desperately want to be listened to, but what we do is just basically talk."

People can tell very easily if you're on automatic pilot and have tuned out. This reveals itself most obviously through unimaginative questioning, or by not responding to something that requires a follow-up. It takes effort to speak effectively, and if the interviewee hears what sounds like a list of questions being rattled off by rote, he or she is not likely to expend a lot of energy responding. An uninterested attitude can also interfere with the interviewee's ability to develop thoughts beyond a superficial level. Nothing is more frustrating to an interviewee than to raise a point that needs a stimulating response to take it further only to have the interviewer abruptly shift the subject in another direction.

When that happens, it signals that you are not truly interested in what the person has to offer, that you're not really "there." Faced with that loud and clear message, many people surrender to the interviewer's standards, figuring that it's hopeless trying to go it alone. Although some will persevere on their own, determined to make their points and represent themselves well despite you, others will lose energy and enthusiasm, and the interview will suffer.

However, when the opposite occurs and you listen deeply, your response assists and inspires the person to speak with more clarity and eloquence. The simple but demanding act of listening with total concentration, which includes hearing more than just the person's words, enables the speaker to concentrate and to reach more deeply for ideas and ways to express them. Because people rarely experience the pleasure and empowerment of being listened to intently, they feel it immediately when it exists. It generates excitement and makes them want to connect with the person who is the source of that enjoyment. The ultimate reward for active listening seems only just: people reciprocate and listen to you. If you find in interviews that you're not taken seriously, improving your listening skills could be one way of changing that.

On a more mundane level, you run many risks by being content to simply keep the conversation moving, with no regard for what is really being said or taking place. The danger is that you'll miss out on the best information and, in so doing, make a fool of yourself. This was demonstrated only too clearly in a broadcast observed by globe-trotting interviewer David Frost:

> I remember watching a show in England once: George Raft was on, and so was a woman, a sort of revue star. Now George Raft is a celebrity and it was his first visit to England, so he was quite a catch. He sat there and said, "There was one time when I was in trouble with the Internal Revenue Department. They said if I didn't pay my back taxes, I might go to jail. Then I got a phone call from Frank Sinatra and Frank said, 'I couldn't bear it if my childhood hero, George Raft, was in trouble. So I'm sending over a check for — let's say — a million dollars. If you can pay it back, do; if not, it doesn't matter.'"
>
> Now, this is a fascinating story, and there are a million things one could ask. But the host turned to the lady and said, "Tell me, have *you* ever had problems with money?" (laughter). And she said something like, "Well, I once lost two shillings in the sweepstakes." Well, you just wanted to hurl something, you were so desperate to hear the rest of the Raft-Sinatra story.

You don't have to be that obtuse for it to become apparent that you're listening poorly, if at all. Veteran journalist Peter Desbarats, who has experience in most aspects of media, is now the Dean of the Graduate School of Journalism at the University of Western Ontario. "I've been interviewed quite a bit in the last few years, particularly when I was working on the Kent Commission [a Royal Commission investigating the concentration of ownership and control of newspapers in Canada]. You can tell rapidly if somebody's just doing it [interviewing] because it's a job, or if he's made up his mind beforehand what you're going to say. Even on the telephone, you get that kind of bored feedback coming back and it really turns you off."

Often at the root of poor listening skills is insecurity: a fear of exploring the unknown and the unpredictable. It's a bit of a gamble to listen deeply, because you may hear or have to respond to certain things you aren't prepared for. Hearing them could force you to abandon a carefully designed game plan, or question the validity of the preconceptions you brought to the interview. It could also draw you farther into a genuine discussion with the guest, during which your limited knowledge or biases might be exposed.

By not listening well, you can deceive yourself into thinking that everything is under control and that your vulnerable areas are protected. If there are topics that make you uncomfortable, you may not hear openings that could take the discussion beyond the safe and superficial. For example, if you're unsure of your sexuality, you may not want to delve past a certain point in a conversation with a psychiatrist about the causes of homosexuality. If you have predetermined notions about your guest or the subject matter, you may unconsciously choose not to hear anything that challenges those ideas, especially if the new information would result in your having to rethink your thesis and do more work on the story.

b. SILENCE IS ELOQUENT

Integral to developing good listening skills is the need to understand and become comfortable with silence. Some interviewers, often out of nervousness, cannot restrain themselves from filling every pause or moment of reflection with the sound of their own voices. This is particularly true in broadcasting where an almost hysterical fear of so-called "dead air" exists. Robert MacNeil, the cohost of *The MacNeil/Lehrer News Hour* on PBS, says this paranoia is unwarranted:

> The hardest thing to do in television is to listen to the answers. The reason is that the interviewer, from his earliest experience, has a terror of dead air, that the answer will be brief and he won't have another question ready. So to cover himself, he starts looking at and getting ready with the next question on his list

almost the minute he's finished asking the one preceding. Just watch interviews very closely on television, and how, before the camera cuts to the interviewee, you'll often see the interviewer's eyes drop to the page right after asking the question.

The difficulty of listening is that you're taking the risk that listening may produce a more interesting question. It might give rise to "Oh, what do you really mean by that?" and a little bit of dead air for a minute. Frankly, we don't care, Lehrer and I, about a little dead air. We'd rather be caught musing for a moment and saying, "Gee, that's interesting. I hadn't thought about that. Let me see, what do I want to ask you next?"

The primary benefit of remaining silent at appropriate times is that, invariably, the guest will continue to speak. It's natural for people to pause and think, especially when they're struggling with a difficult concept or experiencing a release of emotion. If you jump in and cut them off at those crucial times, you're going to stop some important and interesting answers from coming out. That's not to say you let people ramble on until they run out of breath. Profound revelations don't follow every pause. But if you allow moments of brief silence, it's often well worth the wait.

While your silence makes it possible for people who want to keep talking to do so, it also works with guests who prefer to say little. "I always say I earn my living doing two things," says Eric Malling of CBC-TV's investigative program *the fifth estate*. "I earn my money talking to people before the camera rolls and I make my money keeping my mouth shut after it starts to roll. The most important thing about interviewing is knowing when to keep quiet. People hate silence. If somebody answers a question and you can tell they're not quite finished, say nothing and they'll start again. And often what comes out is the real answer."

If you remain silent, it often makes the other person uncomfortable. "I know, personally, that when I'm talking to someone and there's a long silence, I always feel inclined to jump in and break that silence," says Judy Nyman of the *Toronto Star*. "But when I'm interviewing, I don't; and because people feel uncomfortable with silences, they keep talking. And sometimes the best stories or the best leads come from a broken silence when the person feels the need to fill that void, and they'll just start talking."

What goes through the interviewee's unconscious mind during that momentary void is a variation of the following: an interview is a series of questions and answers, with the interviewer charged with the responsibility of knowing when questions are supposed to be asked. If no question is forthcoming, it must be because my answer is inadequate or incomplete. Therefore, I'd better keep talking.

A speaker who's been delivering a contrived response has nothing prepared to fall back on when greeted with silence (it's also useful to give the person a slight smile and subtle nod as reinforcement to keep going). If the speaker takes the plunge and continues to talk, what comes out is likely much closer to the truth. Initially, his or her speech may become clumsier and less articulate. In the grasping for words that tends to accompany the beginning of this second stage of the answer, some valuable information may be obtained by closely observing the struggle to speak. What words or phrases have the most trouble coming out? Is there a clearing of the throat? (It's usually an indication that something is about to be spoken that's not easy for the person to say.) Has the tone of voice or body posture changed?

It's at these key times that slight openings may appear in a guest's armor. Once your guest has begun to dig himself or herself into a hole, prod the person along gently with the right follow-up question until past the point of recovery. Avoid triumphant gestures or aggressive questions at the first hint of an opening. The wrong move could make your guest retreat quickly before any information of substance comes out.

Another benefit of sealed lips is that it can buy time when you can't think of what to say next. A silence in a broadcast interview can seem like an eternity; somewhat less so for print. But it's only a moment, and if you don't fear it, it can help protect you. If you get stuck without a question ready and feel a wave of panic rushing through you, say nothing. Don't fumble for words; you'll only sink deeper into confusion and incoherence. Try to relax, look at the guest, and wait to see what happens. More often than not, you'll be reprieved. The guest will continue to talk, either from that sense of obligation previously mentioned or from having recognized your need for help. If instead your silence produces nothing but a blank stare, don't despair. In stopping for an instant, a question may have popped into your mind. If not, it isn't the end of the world to say you've lost your train of thought. That admission itself will often clear your head, because it relieves some of the panic, or it will prompt the guest to bail you out.

This method produced fascinating results for Pierre Pascau, a widely-experienced Canadian broadcaster who has worked on programs such as *W5* and *the fifth estate*. For the past several years, he's been the host of *L'Informateur*, a daily interview show on CKAC Radio in Montreal that attracts an average daily audience of 226,000 listeners. At the 1985 Centre for Investigative Journalism conference in Toronto, Pascau spoke passionately about his belief that interviewers must be active listeners and intuitive questioners. Instead of relying on formulas, Pascau suggested searching for creative ways of handling difficult situations:

One day I interviewed Mayor Drapeau of Montreal . . . for a municipal election a few years back. I don't know if you know [him], he's a very funny character. He only says what he wants to say and he doesn't say what he doesn't want to say. All kinds of people from the CBC had interviewed him and attacked him because they hated his guts. They wanted to embarrass Drapeau and make him look like a fool and they asked him all kinds of very tough questions. But they made fools of themselves because Drapeau doesn't say what he doesn't want to say.

He called and asked to be on my show. I didn't want him, because it's Drapeau who dominates the media as far as Montreal is concerned. He only talks when he wants to. And I thought, I'm not going to play his game. But I said come [on to my show] anyway.

I introduced him and I said, "This is the Mayor of Montreal, Mr. Jean Drapeau. Okay, Mr. Drapeau, what do you have to say?" And he started talking and he went on [for a while] and I looked at him with a polite smile on my face and I said nothing. And then he said, "Mr. Pascau, you are making faces at me." And I said, "No, Mr. Drapeau, I'm not making faces." "Yes, you are making faces! I can see you making them!" "No, I'm not making . . . " "YES, YOU ARE MAKING FACES!" And I said, "Who would dare make faces at the Mayor of Montreal?" And so he flew into a rage, a tantrum and made a scene, like a spoiled brat, and it was beautiful. You know, it's the nicest interview I ever had with the Mayor of Montreal and I said nothing. I just smiled.

c. AS YOU WERE SAYING . . .

A kindred habit to that of filling in silences is the annoying practice of finishing a speaker's thoughts or sentences. Not only is it aggravating to the guest, it is highly counterproductive for the interviewer, whose purpose is to record other people's words, not his or her own. Finishing a friend's thought, in personal conversation, can at times be a supportive gesture. But in an interview, as Judy Nyman points out, it can be deadening: "I know in my personal life I have a terrible habit of interrupting people when they're speaking. I'll often finish their sentences, and 50% of the time I may be right about what they were going to say. But if you interrupt during an interview, you will often miss the best part of your quote or the best part of your story."

Finishing someone's sentences can be a power game, the object of which is to keep the other person off balance and you in control. To begin with, it diminishes the value of what's being said. How can a speaker feel comfortable and inspired to talk if his or her words and ideas are so predictable and of such little interest that you can't even wait to hear them come out? It also signals your impatience, implying that nothing new or exciting is being said. As well, it disturbs the rhythm of the speaker's thought process. It's hard to maintain a lucid train of thought if someone keeps butting in as you're about to formulate your ideas and conclusions.

These kinds of interjections also serve to shift attention in your direction, so that you become the primary focus of the interview and not the guest. You may want to show off how much you know about the subject, or be overcompensating for not really knowing very much. Or you may be eager to establish your power and let the guest know who's the boss. Whatever the reason, the result is usually negative. Quotes and clips are missed because the answers have been supplied by you instead of the guest. And the speaker may become irritated and confused. An interview, after all, is an invitation for someone to express what he or she knows and thinks about a subject. If you rudely persist in not just asking the questions but also giving the answers, it will only be natural for a guest to become annoyed, and gradually to say less and less.

A more aggressive variation on this theme is to interrupt before the guest has had a decent chance to reply. Such interviewers fire off questions, prefacing them with admonishments such as "Wait a second . . ." or "Are you trying to say . . ." without waiting to hear the answer. This happened to Jean-Claude Parrot, the head of the Canadian Union of Postal Workers, on a talk show in Ottawa in 1978:

> The host was always raising the public against the union, saying we were the scum of the earth, the worst people in society. He introduced me and made a speech about how bad the union was — it was at a time leading up to a strike — and then he started to ask me questions. I would start to answer and he would interrupt. He'd ask another question, I'd start to answer, again he would interrupt. He did this over and over, not giving me a chance to speak.
>
> Fortunately, the program was an hour and a half, because after 20 minutes, when he next did this, I

didn't answer. So he looked at me and asked the question again. And I said, "Look, you're the one who invited me here today. If you don't want me to answer any of your questions, tell me now. You want to say you have me speaking on your show, but you're the only one talking. If you don't want me here, I'll leave."

He didn't know what to do. He asked me another question and then he let me go on and on. I think I spoke for about seven or eight minutes straight. Finally I was able to speak and take calls.

The ultimate extension of this type of bullying, albeit in a much more passive guise, is to monopolize the conversation altogether. One culprit of this practice was Margaret Trudeau, the former wife of the former prime minister, when she co-hosted a morning TV program in Ottawa. Author Christopher Hyde, in an interview with Peter Gzowski on CBC Radio's *Morningside* about life on the book tour, described being a guest on her show:

> We spent about 15 minutes, live, talking about her new artificial fingernails before we ever got around to actually discussing my book. We had a whole discussion about perhaps having Cuisinart fingernails — she runs a cooking segment on the show as well — so that you can have serrated edges so you can chop vegetables with your forefinger.... And then finally, she kind of leaned back and said, "My, you've written an exciting book." And I couldn't help myself. I said, "Did you read it?" She said, "No, actually. But it's supposed to be very exciting."

d. HEARING IS BELIEVING

Cartoonist Lynn Johnston, whose *For Better or Worse* comic strip is syndicated internationally, runs into interviewers who feel the need to compete with their perception of her as a "funny" person. "In print, if interviewers consider themselves very witty or funny, they sometimes interject stuff that you didn't say to try and make the article amusing," she says. "One of them had me saying, '*Mea culpa! Mea culpa!*' Not only didn't I say it, at the time I didn't know what it meant."

It's possible the print reporter actually believed she heard the *mea culpas*. One of the side effects of not listening well is that you tend to hear only what you want to. This can extend to things that weren't said at all, or were spoken in a different context from what you perceived. Not listening can occur either deliberately or unconsciously, especially if you need to hear certain responses to justify or provide a focus for your story. If the reporter in Lynn Johnston's example had decided, ahead of time, that her article was going to be a humorous encounter with a "crazy" cartoonist, then all her radar would be primed to receive material supporting that blueprint. In other words, her projection about the person and the story would have a paramount bearing on what she heard, thought she heard and eventually produced as a record of their conversation together. That's not to rule out the possibility that the reporter may have willfully made up some quotes. But it's also possible that a more subtle process may have been at work.

I've spoken with hundreds of interviewees over the past few years, the vast majority of whom claimed bitterly to have been misquoted and quoted out of context in print interviews. The vast majority of interviewers I've talked with, however, claim the interviewees are crying foul in order to dissociate themselves from accurate quotes that got them into trouble once they were made public. Faced with these opposite responses, there are two possible conclusions: one, that this is a clear-cut case of good guys versus bad guys (choose your side depending on your point of view); or, two, that most of the time there's a problem in the way the two sides are communicating.

One of the busiest Canadian federal government departments as far as media requests for interviews and information are concerned is the Health Protection Branch of Health and Welfare Canada in Ottawa. Jean Sattar, a former media enquiries officer with the department who now works for another ministry, estimates she handled from 200 to 400 separate calls a month, sometimes referring the reporter to the appropriate scientist, sometimes doing the interview herself. The subjects she dealt with were often complicated, involving scientific and technical information. She says she could sense if a reporter was choosing not to listen:

> I talked to the *Ottawa Citizen* in early 1985 about a new study in the [United] States implying there was a definite cause-and-effect link between the use of aspirin and Reye's Syndrome. I was asked leading questions . . . about what we were going to do about the study. I pointed out, first of all, that we hadn't seen the study. Secondly, that it was just another piece of information, but not enough to be the final piece. And, over and over, the fact that you have to base any kind of regulatory decision of industry on a fair body of scientific evidence. But I could feel that the reporter had a particular angle in mind and it didn't matter what I had to say.
>
> The next thing you know, I see the paper and it says something along the line that Health and Welfare was likely going to do such and such, as if the odds were pretty good [that we'd take action]. And I had been very careful to point out that we were completely neutral at that point. It ended up on the CP [Canadian Press] wire and CBC Radio.

Although the reporter was given a clear policy statement by Sattar several times, what came out in print was contrary to that information; and although Sattar could feel the reporter was pursuing that course of action, she never confronted that gut feeling or challenged the line of questioning. Without being judgmental or knowing all the details, I think it's fair to say that, although the onus is overwhelmingly on the reporter to represent the information accurately and fairly, both the reporter and Sattar contributed to the end result: an inaccurate story.

The details of the above situation are far less important than the underlying issues that it raises. Some of the factors that might be at work in such a situation, influencing how the two parties communicate, are listed below. An interview with a government scientist is used as an example.

1. On the interviewer's part

(a) You may have little education in science, find scientists intimidating and regard the subject matter as ungraspable.

(b) Your formal education may be considerably less than that of the scientist, who may also have an office, a secretary, and a good salary, symbols of power and prestige that you may not have.

(c) You may think that people who work for the government are not going to tell the truth, and that they are in collusion with industry to the detriment of public safety.

(d) You may have predetermined your story before doing the interview. This happens for a variety of reasons, the most common being that it's easiest, especially for daily reporting. As one TV reporter explained, "You pretty well have to have the story written before you go to get the clips. There isn't much time for a lot of research." This attitude is less prevalent in print, although it also exists: "This is the story, go get the quotes to back it up."

This attitude also stems from an inherently destructive characteristic of the media — an overwhelming need for black-and-white stories. They're easier to write, easier to read, and can be done quickly. When good versus evil, right versus wrong, or safe versus unsafe are clearly delineated, both the producer and the consumer of the story tend to be much happier. Unfortunately, most protagonists and most issues, when examined closely, turn a shade of gray. That change in color can be a problem. It can result in having to look at the complexities of the issue, which can't be explained in a short article or brief broadcast report. Or, much worse, it could mean the story has to be scrapped because to tell it accurately would take too much time and effort. The safest way to avoid this scenario is to show up with the script already written, ask preset questions, and ignore any answers that would upset your plans.

(e) You may be too nervous or embarrassed to admit you don't know much about the issue, and you think that to have any power during the interview it's best to pretend that you understand what's being said. Hence you nod in agreement to points that, in truth, are confusing. Unsure about what's really being said, you find your only solace in the dogged pursuit of your original angle, no matter how much the interviewee tries to steer you in another direction.

(f) You may interpret these attempts to influence your thinking as an underhanded scheme to divert you away from the real story. The more it happens, the more convinced you become. (You may also be correct, but that's to be determined through research.)

(g) You may have a deadline looming that makes it hard to think beyond just getting the goods as quickly as humanly possible, much less listen effectively.

2. On the interviewee's part

The interviewee —

(a) may have a terrible fear of being interviewed, of having to perform, of having his or her words put on the record.

(b) may have been directed by the minister/department/boss to say nothing of substance, especially opinion or criticism, to the media. The interviewee may share that view.

(c) may think the media is just interested in negative stories, and that they're basically out to make government employees look as bad as possible.

(d) may consider it beneath him or her to have to speak on-the-record with someone who has less education, no knowledge of science, and to whom everything will have to be explained at a Dick-and-Jane level.

(e) may fear being ridiculed by his or her peers if quoted in a superficial article, and may have no interest in sharing information with a public that probably cannot understand it anyway.

(f) may sense that the reporter isn't clear about the story, but not know what, if anything, can be done about it. The thought of questioning the questioner doesn't occur to the interviewee.

(g) may be so hostile and defensive during the interview that no information of any value comes out. When the reporter explains that the story has to be done, with or without the interviewee's cooperation, he or she doesn't care about or understand the possible ramifications of this lack of cooperation.

(h) may be so nervous that he or she hides behind jargon and government doublespeak. No matter how much you try to get your interviewee to provide lay definitions, he or she won't help you out.

These are only some of the factors that could have a bearing on how the interviewer and scientist communicate. The interviewee may also be deliberately withholding information. Considering the complexities, it's no wonder that problems arise. When people are nervous, under pressure, have stereotypical images of each other, and are dealing with difficult subject matter, all this interference can hinder the possibility of listening to each other clearly.

For the interviewer, the way to clear that interference is simple, but difficult to attain. It requires being as honest and perceptive as possible to what's going on during the interview. That means knowing your motivation for doing the story; being aware of your preconceptions, biases, and extent of knowledge; being able and willing to read the guest accurately (for example, is he or she nervous, or being deceitful?); being prepared and relaxed enough to find and follow your instincts during the interview; and monitoring how well you're listening to what's being said.

If you develop these faculties, the result will be more productive and accurate interviews. You'll be more confident about when to be aggressive and when to be sympathetic, because there will be a philosophical base, rather than unthinking, indiscriminate actions, directing your decisions. There's no guarantee that you're always going to make the right moves, by any means, but it's a better foundation to work from than none at all. The chances are much greater that a positive collaboration will result.

e. GRIEVING INDIANS MAKE GOOD PICTURES

The morning after Air-India Flight 182 crashed into the North Atlantic Ocean on June 23, 1985, killing all 329 on board, Richard Gizbert, a news reporter with CFTO-TV in Toronto, was told he'd be on a plane to Cork, Ireland that afternoon to cover the story. I talked to him a few hours before his departure, and it was obvious he felt considerable apprehension about the intensity of what lay ahead. He felt that the media attitude of "grieving Indians make good pictures" meant that he had to find someone at the airport who he could "work" on the plane, even though he wasn't looking forward to getting people to perform in front of the cameras.

I pointed out that this attitude made it easier for him not to look at these people as individuals going through a very difficult time, and also made it easier for him to intrude and ask painful questions when they might just want to be left alone. He asked what else he could do when he had to produce a story.

PM: Maybe what you should do is just sit with him during the flight as a friend. Maybe the best thing to do is say nothing the whole time, if that's what he needs, or talk a blue streak, if that's what he wants. In other words, don't "work" him. Just be with him. If you want him to open up and trust you enough to give you an interview, maybe you've got to connect with him in some real way first.

RG: But the deadlines are going to be murder. I've got to have something planned by the time the plane gets to Cork.

PM: Look, I figure that if you treat him properly, and yourself for that matter, the story will take care of itself.

You'll get your interviews and meet your deadlines. But to me the worst thing you can do, especially for your own peace of mind, is think of him as a "grieving Indian," some disposable product that can be exploited for some clip on the evening news. Now it could be that, as a catharsis, he might really want to talk on television. You won't know that until you spend some time with him.

RG: I see what I'm doing. I'm supposed to do a story on how these people are feeling and I've got it all worked out without considering them.

PM: Right. Because it's not pleasant having to go into a situation where all these people are in mourning or are hysterical, whatever, and ask them questions like, "How do you feel?" along with a mob of other reporters. Some of them are going to scream at you, some are going to break down. You're going to feel like an intruder or that you're exploiting them. No matter what happens, you're going to be affected by the whole scene and energy there.

But you also have a job to do. I figure the only way to survive it is to feel right about what you're doing. That means dealing with these people on a personal level and using your instincts to know who and when to approach. If you handle it that way, you can still meet your deadlines and you'll probably get more powerful clips from people because they'll be more willing to talk to you. And the bottom line is, you'll still like yourself when it's over.

f. SAYING NOTHING TIRED ME OUT

Active listening requires all your energy, according to Roy MacGregor of the *Ottawa Citizen*, one of Canada's top feature writers. His strength in an interview, where his style is quiet and supportive, is to get people to trust and confide in him:

> I can go out and interview someone for an hour and that person will have the sense of being with someone

who is uncommonly comfortable. They are confronted by someone who is sitting there in a completely relaxed state of mind, who seems on the verge of falling asleep.

But I go out of the interview completely exhausted. I have to go home and go to sleep. What I'm doing is that inside I am churning so fast, it's as if I'm playing 19 games of squash. I'm just beat. And yet my body gives off a sense of total relaxation. I don't know how, because I'm not relaxed. I am trying to remember things, remember what I have to return to. And I am trying to act like it is just a casual conversation and much of it doesn't matter. Even though all of it matters.

This combination of complete attention and seeming repose seduces the interviewee into a sense of intimacy, where anything can be said or revealed without fear of ridicule or rejection. Says MacGregor: "In a long interview, most people seem to fall into a very relaxed state, which is, I presume, what a psychiatrist aims for. And then it becomes shoes off, relaxing the way you would on a very idle evening with an old friend."

For the broadcast interview, the need to listen attentively is paramount. Unlike print, where poorly worded questions, elliptical responses, tones of voice, body language, or manipulative games are lost or deleted in the editing process, everything is exposed in a live broadcast. Even with the luxury of editing, it is not always possible to eliminate your mistakes and excesses. Whereas in print and magazine interviewing the only real goal is to elicit information and quotes, in broadcasting you also need to perform.

The broadcast interview is a form of theater played out on the public stage. In many ways, the performance outshadows the content, placing great pressure on the interviewer to be animated and attractive while also sounding intelligent. Two other factors add stress. One is time, which is usually limited. The other is the need for the interview to flow in a logical order. This latter point is crucial; like theater, a broadcast interview must unfold in a sequence that an audience can follow in one sitting. This demands that the interviewer's system be on red alert, for many complicated choices have to be made simultaneously and publicly. As Terence McKenna, a documentary maker with CBC-TV's *The Journal* explains, there are numerous different commands firing in your brain at the same time, testing your ability to listen:

There's terrific pressure on you to achieve the objectives of the interview. You're trying to stay ahead of yourself. You're trying to think of where his [the guest's] answers are going, where your questions are going. You're trying to think of the precise wording of the next question and you're trying to make sure that no point is left unturned. You're trying to listen to him, making sure that he doesn't present you with an opening in his answer that will go unnoticed because you're concentrating on something else.

Longtime journalist Warner Troyer, who worked on television public affairs programs such as *This Hour Has Seven Days*, *the fifth estate*, and *W5*, says he is "living on pure adrenalin" during a TV interview. He describes the effect this has upon him in metaphysical terms:

I know that when I'm doing a TV interview, and sometimes radio, that if I wanted to at any given moment, I could get up, stroll across the studio, pinch the interviewee's cheek, and walk back and sit down again in a leisurely fashion between any two words he speaks. I know I could, no question about it. It's like H. G. Wells' *Time Machine* story. The clock would stop. Because I'm burning so much adrenalin, everything is happening in slow motion for me.

And that means I have masses of time to listen to what is being said to me, to watch the way it's being said, and to judge the temperature and barometric pressure, intellectually and emotionally, of the person I'm talking to. Based on all of that information and on my imperatives — the things I want to get done and the amount of time left — I can then determine what kind of question I should ask next, what the tone of it should be, whether I should smile or look rather stern, whether I should lean back or forward. [I can determine] whether I'm going to get the kind of response I want to, maybe not to the next question, but to the third one after that you're building toward. It's like defensive driving. You don't look at the car in front of you, you look at the one three cars ahead.

It's not just that you have to *be* there — the rest of the world does not exist. You're in a submarine, a bathysphere, alone with that individual. And you force them to attend to you and only you. And you do force them, with eye contact, with the urgency of your interest in them, all these things.

Listening skills usually improve with experience. As you become more relaxed, more capable of assimilating the various interviewing functions, time starts to slow down, freeing you to listen more deeply. But it is not axiomatic that such a progression will occur. Many seasoned interviewers never evolve to that stage. David Frost told *Playboy* that he was once interviewed on radio by an experienced interviewer who wasn't listening to him at all. "So, for my amusement," Frost said, "I ended an answer by saying, 'And then, of course, I married the Pope's first wife.' And the guy *still* said, 'Yes, yes, Mr. Frost, but what about the Common Market? Do you think butter tariffs will eventually increase?' "

FEATURE INTERVIEW: Dr. Herbert Pollack

Dr. Herbert Pollack is a psychologist at the Clarke Institute of Psychiatry in Toronto. A specialist in communication skills, he's the type of person who, within minutes of meeting him, you feel you could tell anything. He was interviewed by freelance journalist Kim Levis:

KL: What makes a good listener?

HP: Well, someone who wants to listen. I think that's the first thing. You have to want to be there, to value it. Lots of people I know in the communications business aren't really good listeners, even though they know they're supposed to be. They're still busy being good talkers. Or they're trying to impress. Instead of listening, they're saying, "Well, how am I going to respond in a way that will make *me* look good?"

To be a good listener, you have to be aware of what's in it for the other person. You can't only be in tune with your own needs, in terms of what you're going to get from it. You really need to give over the communication to the other person. That's the thing that differentiates the pros from the amateurs. The pros really do this and the amateurs don't. They don't really attend to the other person. [As a pro] you're there for them. Your needs are not as important.

KL: What are some other things that come into play?

HP: Particularly in my line of work, where you have people coming in with very complicated problems, they may be saying one thing but underneath they're saying something else. And you've got to be attuned to their tone of voice, to very subtle nuances [such as] looking away or looking down. Or sometimes, when people are talking, they'll swallow a word, indicating some discomfort. It won't sound congruent. The words and the music won't be together. They'll be saying something, but it doesn't jibe with the music that's coming out, either in terms of the tone of voice or the eye contact.

It's something that's very difficult to teach, the ability to "listen with the third ear," as some people call it. This is what Wilhelm Reich, who was an analyst, talked about. [It involves] not just hearing the words but hearing the music in the words. I don't know if that's an image that's helpful to you, but it's helpful to me.

KL: How about things like crossing arms to form a barrier?

HP: I think that's overdone, actually. I think it's more up here [points to head]. It's a sense you get. If you're in love with someone, you know when things are good and you know when things start going bad. It's not necessarily because they are crossing their arms; there's a whole kind of ambience that you have to be sensitive to. And to be a good listener, you have to be sensitive to this sort of ambience.

I know that a lot of people will go into a communication situation and say, "Aha. This person is sitting this way and that means he's defensive." It's just a lot of crap. I think it's overdone. You know, sometimes people sit that way because that's the way they sit. It's really up here [points to eyes] and up here [points to ears] and down here [points to heart] that you feel if the other person is really listening.

KL: So it's really an instinct?

HP: Yeah. The other thing you have to do is check it out. I mean, *you* may be listening with everything you've got, but if the other person doesn't feel that, you've got to check it out. We advise people to do things like paraphrase. "Let me just check what you said. This is what I heard. Is that what you said?" You want to make sure that the message you're getting is really what was being said. And you want to make sure that the message you're sending is what the other person is getting. So a good listener asks: "Does the other person understand what I'm saying?"

KL: Do you find a difference between how men and women listen?

HP: I think in general women are better listeners because in our culture women certainly have been trained to be more sensitive. And I think in order to be a good listener, you have to be sensitive and to have developed more social skills. Now whether that's changing or not . . . it possibly is.

More women go into therapy and women tend to be better therapists because they're more willing to admit their weaknesses. Whereas some men are into this macho trip — to admit to flaws is not being a man.

KL: So when you are advising men on how to listen, what do you tell them?

HP: Not to be ashamed of their emotions. If you're having an emotional reaction to someone, that means something other than, "Uh-oh, I'm not supposed to be [having a reaction]. Let's forget about that." [Instead] spend a minute saying, "Hey, what's going on inside me?" And [I tell them] to be more sensitive to their own feelings, not to disguise or distort them or sweep them under the rug.

KL: Is interviewing an art or a science?

HP: You can look at it as either an art or a science or both. I think the public would like to believe that we really could have an equation and that it's basically a skill — anybody can pick it up. And to some extent, that's true. I'm not sure to what extent — maybe 30-40-50 percent.

The other part is instinct; taking risks; feeling good enough about yourself to ask a stupid question, which may turn out to be a very creative question. But you can't play it safe. You have to let yourself go. You have to trust your emotions and you have to do it on the spot. And if you make a mistake, so what? It's not the end of the world.

So people who are perfectionists or not spontaneous would have a hell of a time. Because once the person you're interviewing breaks the rules or doesn't want to follow your particular outline, what are you going to say? "Well, gee, you gotta follow this outline." You have to go with it, and you have to be prepared to go wherever it goes. Go on a journey, and some journeys end happily and some don't. But when they don't end happily, then hopefully you've learned something. So you'll say, "OK, that interview didn't go well. Why? Well, it was clear we didn't get off on the right foot. My first question pissed him off. And from there it was all downhill. I had a chance to turn it around, but I decided to play it safe. And we didn't establish a rapport." But you have to establish a rapport, and to do that you have to be prepared to break the rules, gamble a little, go for it.

2

THE ELEMENTS OF RESEARCH

There are few worse feelings than the flush of mortification that overcomes you when your ignorance is exposed during an interview. Apart from the deflating effect it can have upon your confidence and ability to continue, it can also diminish your credibility, shift the balance of power, and destroy whatever degree of intimacy you may have established with the guest. If it's apparent that you're unprepared or know little about the subject, an interviewee will likely become — with justification — irritated, uncooperative or condescending, or will simply attempt to take control.

In an article he wrote for *TV Guide* following the dismal failure of his talk show, *In the Thicke of the Night*, Alan Thicke provided an example of the humiliating predicament you can find yourself in when you don't have the right information. Although he didn't elaborate on the specific ramifications of this brief exchange with actor Keith Carradine, it's not hard to imagine the pall that the question cast upon the rest of their discussion:

AT: Your dad was such a great actor, we're all saddened by his passing.
KC: My father's still alive.
AT: Oh, how's he feeling?

Although Carradine didn't stomp off the set, vacuous or insulting questions — particularly those posed in a public setting like a scrum or news conference — can upset the guest enough to result in the termination of the interview. A legendary example is the question posed to Vivien Leigh when she arrived in Atlanta for the re-release of *Gone With The Wind* on its twentieth anniversary. "What role did you play?" a dullard of a reporter enquired of the great star. "Look it up, sonny," was her icy reply. The interviewer turned scarlet and Scarlett turned away.

"It's the inexperienced, unprepared, and stupid reporters who scare me the most," a business executive said during an off-the-cuff discussion of the media. "You don't mind if people are tough, as long as they know what they're doing. But the ones who just fire questions off without thinking make me nervous. I become very cautious about what I say. I don't open up because I don't trust them."

That point was reiterated by author Pierre Berton when he described his worst experience being interviewed. "Do you write your own books?" a reporter in Lindsay, Ontario, once asked the irascible Berton, who has about 30 major works to his credit. "How can you treat that kind of person seriously?" Berton says, traces of irritation in his voice. "How can you feel confident about what kind of story will come out?"

Television is considered the worst offender for sending out interviewers who have little knowledge of their subject. With so much emphasis on appearance and packaging, content is often assigned to a distant back seat. In her insightful book, *Mediaspeak: How Television Makes Up Your Mind*, author Donna Woolfolk Cross reports that "A former anchorwoman for WABC-TV in New York was hired even though her only previous experience was as a California model. She recently admitted she once interviewed Henry Kissinger without even knowing who he was!"

If you're unprepared, it soon becomes obvious. Comedian Jerry Lewis, in an interview with CBC Radio's Jim Wright, said it's not hard to tell who hasn't done any homework. (Contrary to expectations, Wright found Lewis to be "totally professional: he was intelligent, cooperative and attentive.")

> The first question they ask is, "So, Jerry, what brings you to town?" I have no patience for that kind of person. He's lazy, he doesn't like his job, he doesn't

like you. And what upsets me the most is that there's a kid out there who would give his eyeteeth to have his job. I say to him, "Look, you've got just two minutes and at the end of those two minutes I'm walking out of here because you're a jerk, you're obviously not prepared and you're wasting my time." And then the guy goes away and writes what a jerk *I* am.

A journalist must at the very least know the basics about a potential interviewee. That seems so obvious as to be not worth stating, but I began to wonder when I saw the results of a series of current affairs tests I gave my first year journalism students in 1985. About 80% couldn't name the current Governor-General. The same percentage failed to identify more than two of the ten provincial premiers, while many spelled the surname of their own province's leader, then William Davis, as "Davies." Few knew what the term "federal cabinet" meant; those who did could identify only two ministers on average.

a. THE PURPOSE OF RESEARCH

Research is done for two main reasons: to allow the interviewer to understand a story and ask intelligent and probing questions; and to let the interviewer relax by increasing confidence, which helps the interviewer's intuition and instincts to work at their highest capacity.

If you shun preparation and choose to "wing" interviews, you might sometimes get by on curiosity, good listening skills, and acute intuition. But that will only take you so far. I can see no logical argument for knowing little or nothing about a subject that you're about to discuss with someone who probably knows a great deal. Without your own sources of information, you're at the mercy of whatever the interviewee tells you. Although there are exceptions, in most cases the guest will know more about the subject at hand than you. Research allows you to offset that imbalance and engage the guest in conversation at a more equal and stimulating level.

But at the same time an interview is far more than just a series of questions. Not only should you be concerned with what the guest is saying, you must be totally alert to what is *not* said, the tone in which questions are answered, non-verbal communications, and any psychological games being played. In other words, you must be aware of the emotional as well as the intellectual levels of the interview. In order to decide whether a guest is in need of a gentle approach or an aggressive push you must make decisions based on far more than just what's being said. To do so effectively and with confidence, your instincts must be finely tuned.

The better prepared you are, the greater the chance of that happening. If your mind is racing helter-skelter, searching for questions or trying to comprehend what the interview is really about, you won't be relaxed enough to do much more than survive. If you're thoroughly prepared, however, you'll be more able to connect with the guest — and understand the subject matter — on a deeper level. Needless to say, there's more to developing your instinctive qualities than just doing research. But the confidence provided by the research will free you to gamble and experiment more, to break down the structure of formal questions-and-answers and engage in a genuine conversation.

These two main reasons for doing research can be broken down into a number of subsidiary reasons.

1. It informs you about the topic and the guest.

How can you discuss nuclear energy with a scientist if you don't know fusion from fission? How can you do a biographical interview with a movie star if you know nothing about the star's background or films?

A little bit of digging about actor Sylvester Stallone, for example, turns up that he has an autistic child (which may help to explain why he downplays dialogue in his films) and that he believes very seriously in reincarnation — he's certain that in a past life he was beheaded during the French Revolution. If your objective is to look past the stereotypical Rocky-Rambo image, this information could help to achieve that goal.

The extent of your research depends entirely on the complexity of the topic, the space allotted to your story, the deadline you must meet, and the resources on hand to do the work. Often, there will be little need or opportunity to do more than a brief amount of research, if any. This is especially the case in daily reporting, where stories have to be covered quickly.

It's important, however, not to use an impending deadline as an excuse to avoid preparation. This is a habit that's easy to fall into, but one that will limit the quality of your work. Once you've overcome the initial jitters about doing interviews, it's not difficult to get by on a fairly stock number of questions that don't require much thought or homework. While that might be adequate for some situations, it will rarely take your work beyond the mundane or predictable. Powerful interviews can happen spontaneously by relying on nothing but your listening skills and intellect, but the odds are not in your favor. Over the long run, hard work will produce higher and more consistent results.

2. It enables you to prepare informed, challenging, and creative questions.

Without research, the scope of your knowledge is severely restricted. If you aren't aware of pivotal events in the interviewee's life, key anecdotes, or the background to the issues, how can you ask about them? Granted, the guest may volunteer some of this information, but there's no guarantee. People tend to be very polite in interviews, just answering what they're asked. Therefore, if your questions are of a broad and exploratory nature, you're inviting the same in return.

3. It eliminates the need to ask unnecessary questions, especially if your time with the interviewee is limited.

Basic material such as biographical data or the history of an issue can be obtained elsewhere, freeing you to make the most of whatever time is available. Unnecessary questions are also irritating to people who are frequently interviewed and are tired of having to regurgitate the same old stories.

A frequent complaint of scientists or people involved with technical subjects is that the task of doing *your* homework is foisted onto them before the interview can begin. Sometimes that is unavoidable, as the interview itself serves as the starting point of your research. Even when that's the case, though, you should endeavor to read and learn as much about the subject as is reasonable so that you at least have a rudimentary understanding. That will also show the guest that you don't expect him or her to do all the work.

4. It can help streamline the interview process, identifying very specifically the areas to be covered with a particular guest.

"If all you need is a lobster, there's no point coming home with a net also full of mackerel, smelts, and squid," says Stuart McLean. "If your research shows that all you'll get from a professor, for example, is the physical description of a piece of machinery, then better to spend all your energy getting that from him as best as possible than wasting time asking questions about things you'll never use."

5. It is essential for adversarial interviews.

Unless you know as much, if not more, than a person you expect will lie, distort, or evade an issue, you're powerless. Often there's a testing period in these types of encounters, where the guest will challenge your facts and understanding of the story. This situation came up in an interview I did with David Hume, the President of Oshawa General Hospital, for an article for *Toronto Life* magazine about an operation at the hospital that had gone wrong. It was alleged that an anesthetist had been doing a crossword puzzle during the operation, resulting in the retardation and physical disability of the patient. At one point during our fairly strained first meeting, Hume responded to some tough questions by challenging me about how much I knew about the demanding conditions anesthetists work under during a long operation. It was a crucial moment, for my credibility was on the line. If I just took educated guesses, he could attack me on several fronts, shifting the focus of the interview onto my lack of knowledge, preparation, and professionalism. He could even use it as an excuse to discontinue the interview. No matter what course of action he chose, I would have lost power and he would have gained. However, because I was able to reply that I had spoken to several leading experts in the field, including someone he knew personally, the opposite effect occurred. From that point on, our conversation became less confrontational. Knowing that he couldn't intimidate or bamboozle me, he began to explain rather than attack. The result was better for both of us. More information came out, in a clearer form, and the atmosphere became less tense.

Similar moments arise in interviews of all types, from confrontational to sweetheart. If a guest suspects or has witnessed the limitations of your knowledge, he or she will likely lose respect or interest, or feel more confident playing whatever game, whether bullying or patronizing, that suits his or her purpose.

6. It can place the story and/or the guest in an historical or contextual perspective.

It is important to understand the evolution of a political philosophy or party, an economic policy or social legislation, and the major players who are or have been the exponents of those ideals. In the current affairs quiz I gave my journalism students, almost none could name the year the War Measures Act was imposed or the year the Parti Québecois came to power. Many weren't even close, being decades off. What was more disturbing, though, was a general attitude that this information wasn't necessary. Everything existed in the moment, so that stories weren't looked at in context but simply as one-time events. This attitude was reflected in their approach to research, which was done with great reluctance. Understanding a story was secondary by far to getting it on the air (an attitude, I should say, that journalism schools contribute to greatly).

7. It's a form of respect and flattery.

Your research tells the guest that you cared enough and considered him or her important enough to do some homework. This is of particular benefit if you unearthed information that produces stimulating rather than predictable questions. Many of the people you interview will have little time to waste. If you arrive uninformed, they may perceive that as disrespect or lack of professionalism, which may endanger the interview's success. People like to be recognized for who they are and what they have accomplished, and they usually like to talk about those subjects.

8. It's one of the ways to establish trust and create a bond with a guest, especially if what's to be discussed is very sensitive.

If you're interviewing a child abuser for a program that's examining the problem and you think that all child abusers are horrible monsters who should be locked up without any questions asked, that attitude is likely going to make it hard for the interviewee to open up. If in doing research, however, you discover that most child abusers were themselves abused and that the behavior is basically learned, your questions and tone may shift from being judgmental to compassionate (which doesn't mean to condone but to understand). That change then allows the guest to speak without fear of being ridiculed or condemned. If a guest believes you are a sensitive and trustworthy soul, he or she is more likely to reveal true feelings.

At the same time, you have to be careful not to develop an automatically sympathetic response to someone just because he or she seems willing to discuss feelings. The outpouring of what appears to be genuine emotion is very seductive to journalists, especially in the electronic media. Human behavior is extremely complex, and it's easy to get tricked by someone who seems to be baring his or her soul. The best protection, first of all, is to be aware that it can happen; then it's a case of trusting your instincts. Ask yourself if the response seems genuine or if it is a ruse to keep from exploring the subject matter further.

However sensitive the research work is, however, it can be completely undercut by the actual interview. When Randy Newman's satirical song "Short People," came out, the controversy it provoked resulted in a decision by a radio program I worked for to do a feature on what it's like to be an extremely short male or an exceptionally tall female. After considerable digging, our researcher found two people willing to talk. She assured them, through her tactful negotiation over the telephone, that they'd be treated with dignity. The interview was presented as an opportunity for them to make the public aware of the prejudices faced by people outside the physical norm.

Our host was a tall male in his late thirties. Although he could be insensitive — his own feelings seemed blocked, and interviews dealing with anything emotional tended to make him uncomfortable — no one anticipated a problem with what we presumed would be a straightforward interview.

His first question was to the tall, thin woman. After a bumbling preamble, in which his discomfort with the subject became apparent, he blurted out, "What was it like growing up like a redwood tree?"

The woman was completely taken aback. The interviewer's mocking language echoed the taunts she had heard and sensed all her life. Her voice became strained and she struggled to maintain her composure. Consequently, she tightened up and didn't divulge many of the more profound insights she'd mentioned to the researcher over the phone. Any possibility of a trusting relationship between the two was shattered by the opening question. It also had negative repercussions on the exchange between the host and the short male. That portion of the interview didn't achieve its potential either.

b. IN PRAISE OF LIBRARIES

Perhaps it's a distrust of anything free that makes libraries one of the best-kept secrets in the world of research. It's a terrible shame, because libraries contain a wealth of information, and provide the place to start for many stories.

"I believe you should begin research in the library, with an academic, scholarly approach," says Jim Dubro, a freelance investigative journalist with a solid academic background in eighteenth century English literature. Dubro was a key member of the team that put together the CBC-TV *Connections* series in the late seventies, a dramatic documentation of organized crime in Canada. As the primary researcher, Dubro spent years assembling and cross-referencing files and developing sources on the Byzantine workings of the various crime organizations operating in the country.

"Read everything you can get your hands on: books, articles, government reports," he says. "Three areas in particular are worth looking at carefully: acknowledgments, footnotes, and bibliographies. We found Vinnie Teresa [former mobster who had turned witness for the U.S. government] that way. He'd gone into hiding and no one would tell us where he was. But he'd written a book (*My Life in the Mafia*) and three names were mentioned in the acknowledgments. I tracked these people down . . . left messages that I wanted to talk with Vinnie . . . and eventually he called."

As fond of the academic route as he is, Dubro warns that it's just one path that can be taken. "There's a whole school of investigative journalists who say, forget about people because it's all in the documents. I. F. Stone is of that group. But I don't agree. Maybe 99% of the information is there [in the documents], but it's people who can tell you what documents to look at, where to find certain people, how to interpret the information that exists on paper, how to visualize the story. The two [research and people] should go hand-in-hand."

Whether you're embarking on research for a long-term project or the briefest of articles, there will be information of use to you somewhere in the library. To the uninitiated, however, it can seem an imposing labyrinth. The Metropolitan Toronto (Reference) Library has almost 1.5 million books, while the central building of the New York Public Library has some 80 miles of bookshelves. But finding your way through the maze is not that difficult once you've taken the initial plunge. As long as you're willing to ask for help, and have patience, you should eventually find what you need. To ease the pain of those first steps, here are some guidelines, culled from many years of roaming the aisles.

(a) Bear in mind that it's the librarian's job to assist you. Librarians are trained, knowledgeable people who usually enjoy the challenge of tracking down information, no matter how obscure. Sometimes this can be accomplished over the telephone, if the request is not too complicated. Even if you get flustered, hang in there until you are sure all avenues have been checked.

(b) Don't be afraid to ask questions. Librarians are used to being asked the most elementary questions concerning the workings of their system. No matter how dumb the question, they've heard it before.

(c) Start at the main reference desk. You will probably be directed to a specific section. Obviously, the clearer you are beforehand about what information you require, the easier it will be for the librarian to help. Take the time to make that initial effort.

(d) Use the back issues of the newspapers and magazines (periodicals) that the library subscribes to (either original copies or on microfilm). There will be occasions when you'll have to endure the laborious process of searching through them for information.

(e) Ask about the many indexes that can direct you toward the exact date and source of information you require. Brian Land, one of Canada's leading librarians, explained their usefulness in Stephen Overbury's *Finding Canadian Facts Fast*:

> Indexes are extremely valuable in any kind of library research, and yet I have found that even first-year

university students are unaware of the most standard indexes. The most basic indexes in the country are the *Canadian Periodical Index*, the *Canadian News Index*, the *Canadian Business Index*, and the *Microlog Index* (a monthly listing of reports published by all levels of government and institutions). They cover most Canadian newspapers, magazines, journals, and government and business reports.

Indexes are being offered increasingly through on-line computer services. But computerization really only started in the late 1960s, which means that you still have to do manual searches if you wish to locate publications before this period. There are directories that tell you if a particular publication has been indexed, the most notable of which is *Ulrich's International Periodicals Directory*, which covers Canadian publications. Also, local community libraries often undertake the tedious process of indexing their home town papers.

(f) Don't be intimidated by the microfiche or on-line computer catalogue systems. They may not be as familiar as the old card drawers, but they are much faster and easier to use when you get the hang of them, which doesn't take long. Some of the computer services available can save you an incredible amount of time.

(g) Don't neglect the multitude of reference books that are available. These include old familiars such as encyclopedias, atlases, almanacs, and *Who's Who*. Among the less well-known are the *Corpus Administrative Index*, which is a list of key people in the Canadian federal government along with their telephone numbers, the *Directory of Labour Organizations in Canada*, which includes information on national and international unions, and the *Directory of Associations in Canada*, which is self-explanatory. The list of valuable reference books is endless. Take it for granted that if there's something you need to know, there will be a book in the library that fits your needs.

(h) Government documents of all kinds, such as debates, journals and sessional papers, are available in the larger libraries.

(i) All major libraries will have current telephone directories of Canadian, American, and some major world cities, as well as some government directories. The extent of the collection depends on the library. If you need to find an old directory, ask the librarian. Larger libraries do store them.

(j) Don't restrict your search to public libraries. Universities, colleges, governments, industries, associations, magazines, and the CBC all have libraries, and anywhere else where there's a need to have information stored and catalogued. Not all are accessible to the public, but if you're involved in legitimate research you can often gain access.

(k) Computer searches on a topic are often available for a nominal charge. For example, if you're writing an article on anabolic steroids, the Sport Information Resource Centre (SIRC) in Ottawa (a federal government-funded library) will do a computer search. The computer printout will list articles on the subject and tell you whether the library has a copy. A similar service is offered by Canadian Press and InfoGlobe, providing access to all their newspaper references to a particular subject. Get an estimate of the cost beforehand because some services can be quite expensive.

(l) You don't have to restrict your research to print material. Many film/tape/audio libraries now exist, such as the National Film Board's library or the federal government's Sound Archives in Ottawa.

(m) Finally, be prepared to spend time, often fruitless or painstaking, in your quest to unearth material.

c. REACH OUT AND TOUCH SOMEONE

Because so much research and interviewing is done over the telephone, it's valuable to understand the dynamics involved. Some people, interviewers and guests alike, don't like the telephone, saying it's too impersonal or cold a medium for real communication to take place. The fact that you can't see who you're talking to or how they're reacting is usually mentioned as the main reason for the discomfort. However, that drawback can be used to your advantage. For many journalists, the telephone is the most vital and irreplaceable tool of the trade for the following reasons:

1. Its most endearing quality is speed.

You can accomplish a great deal in a short time, without travel or the social formalities that prolong face-to-face encounters. If you visit someone's home or office, it's hard to pop in, grab a few answers and exit while the coffee is still brewing. "The telephone was my main weapon in print," says Roger Smith, talking about his years as a reporter at Canadian Press. "You could kiss off an interview in 10 minutes — maybe do six good interviews in an hour."

2. You can wrap up the conversation easily and quickly.

If the person turns out to have little information or is hopelessly dull, you can say, "Thank you for your help. I think I may have to go to another source for what I'm looking for." In person, it's always more difficult to depart abruptly. Valuable time can be consumed in the company of people who are not the right contacts, or are lonely, long-winded, and expert at ignoring all signals that you want to leave. There's also the time wasted travelling.

3. The telephone conversation can serve as a screening process for in-person interviews.

A brief pre-interview should allow you to assess whether it's worthwhile meeting the guest.

4. People's sense of time seems to alter when they're caught up in an interesting discussion on the phone.

While you're able to cut dead-end phone interviews short, calls that turn out to be useful often go on much longer than the interviewee imagines. A lengthy conversation can take place without them being aware of it.

5. North Americans are used to talking and divulging information on the phone.

Like revealing secrets to a priest in the confessional, the phone seems to offer a (false) sense of protection and anonymity. "It's like talking to someone on an airplane or in a bar," says Richard Handler, a producer at CBC Radio. "They'll pour their hearts out to you, a stranger, and tell you things they wouldn't tell their wife or husband or best friend."

The success of telephone distress centers, radio phone-in shows dealing with sex and counselling problems, and market research into personal and financial information by phone, shows the willingness of people to answer intimate and probing questions over the phone. For journalism interviews, because the notebook or tape recorder isn't visible, there's usually a more conversational or informal atmosphere, as if the talk is off-the-record, even though it's not. Ironically, the apparent informality also makes it possible to have far more detailed and extensive notes and questions at your disposal.

6. The phone can neutralize some of the power games that can occur when people talk to each other in person.

If an interviewee is physically attractive, much taller, smaller, older or younger than you, extremely shy or aggressive, expensively dressed, or has a lavish home or office, such factors — and many others — can affect how you communicate. And the guest responds to the same things in you. The telephone eliminates those problems and focuses instead on the voice — what is said, how it's said, and how it's received. If, however, you rely on these characteristics as the source of your power, you may not find the phone so appealing.

7. The phone can camouflage your insecurities in meeting people face-to-face.

"I like the phone because you can't see my face," says Larry Zolf, who has stalked the corridors of CBC-TV for more than two decades, performing various on-air and production roles. He has thick glasses and a "sad sack" appearance. "I'm one of the best on the phone. I'm very funny. I trade information. Look, I'll give you something, tell a story in return for what you know. There's an automatic equality between the phoner and the phonee, whoever he is. I'm a very nervous person and on the phone I'm less nervous, or they can't see my nervousness."

There are three basic rules of telephone research:

(a) Don't say you understand something unless you do.

(b) Don't be afraid or unwilling to call people back as often as necessary to verify that something is accurate or clear.

(c) Give people a reason for talking to you. It could be to get exposure for themselves or their cause, to set the record straight, for revenge, glamor, public or personal responsibility, or even money.

Here are some pointers to keep in mind when conducting your telephone interviews:

(a) When contacting people at home, consider carefully the best time to call. This tip doesn't apply to breaking stories, where social niceties take second place to the need for immediacy, no matter what time of day. But if there's a choice, decide if there's a strategic advantage to phoning at a particular time. I prefer to phone between 8 p.m. and 10 p.m., when supper is probably out of the way and it's still not that late. I don't like interviewing early in the morning, but that can be a good time to catch someone at home to make an appointment for later in the day, especially if it's someone you've been having trouble reaching at the office. If you don't have a home number, try calling at work from 7 a.m. on. Many busy people are early risers, and go to the office before secretaries and other personnel arrive. If you wait until after 9 a.m. when the rush starts, you run the risk of getting the "He's in a meeting . . ." and "Can she call you back . . ." blues.

(b) Try to create a conversational mood. People will be far more open and receptive if they don't feel they're being interrogated. Rather than emphasize that you're calling up for an "interview," better to say that you're working on a story and wonder if it would be okay to talk with him or her for a few minutes. If you can mention the name of a mutual acquaintance — even if it's only someone you've interviewed and may not even have met — it can help alleviate some of the suspicion and work toward winning the person's confidence. "Why are you calling me? How did you get my number?" people often ask at the outset. If you can reply, "I was speaking with Jack Swackhammer, who gave me your number and suggested I call you because you're the expert . . . ," it acts almost as a personal reference.

(c) Keep in mind that some people just don't feel comfortable on the telephone. Discomfort on the telephone can be a cultural characteristic, as with the British, for example. Many Britons, accustomed to poor telephone quality and a fee for each call (not to mention their natural reserve) are reluctant to discuss anything but the most basic details except in person. When John Keyes of *TV Guide* was in London for the wedding of Prince Charles and Lady Diana in 1981, he was frustrated at having to take taxis halfway across London to do brief interviews that could have been wrapped up on the phone in a few minutes back home.

Marty York, an aggressive sports reporter with the *Globe and Mail*, does most of his digging over the phone. Convincing professional athletes to talk isn't easy at the best of times these days, but it's especially hard if just being seen with the reporter is enough to get you in hot water with management. York says the telephone makes his job much easier:

> My personal tactic is to use the telephone. That's when they [the players] feel most comfortable. They can say whatever they want and not worry about who's listening. You have to meet them [initially] face-to-face so they know who they're talking to, but after that they feel most comfortable on the phone. If they want to confide in you, they confide in you that way. They don't even want to be seen with you sometimes because they wonder if the other guy thinks they may be telling you something they shouldn't be.

41

If I have a forte, it's on the phone. That's where I get most of my stories. I have two at home and three on my desk at the *Globe* [*and Mail*].

It's important to remember that a personal encounter is potentially more dynamic than one on the phone. It's easy to become lazy and pick up the phone instead of making the effort to visit. Use the phone when it's appropriate, not as force of habit.

d. FROM THE OUTSIDE IN

When researching a profile, the methodology is "to work from the outside in," according to Richard Gwyn. "You work with all your secondary and tertiary sources first, accumulating information, anecdotes, and so on. The last person you usually talk to is the person you're profiling."

The idea is to piece together a history and character sketch of the person you're profiling, discovering him or her through other people's eyes. If you relied solely on what the subject volunteered, the range and depth of your information would be tremendously restricted. You would encounter memory lags, selective omissions, and distortions. Everything would be colored the way the person wished to present it. Instead of having specific questions designed to trigger predetermined, relevant material, you would have to go on a long fishing trip, one in which the prey's cooperation would be paramount just to acquire the most fundamental facts.

"I always ask [the subject] for a list of friends and enemies," says Sandra Gwyn, who writes primarily for *Saturday Night* magazine. "I'm quite upfront about it, and they usually provide them because they understand why you need them. You then interview these people for information and clues to help you understand the person you're writing about." Gwyn used this most effectively for a *Saturday Night* profile she prepared on Joe Clark, soon after he became leader of the Progressive Conservative Party in 1976:

One person I talked to was an old girlfriend of his who said, "He once sent me two books which he felt I should read. One was *Wind in the Willows* and the other was *Slouching Towards Bethlehem* by Joan Didion." Now that was very interesting, because Joan Didion happens to be one of my favorite authors.

I also talked to a friend of mine who happened to be at the University of Alberta with him. She told me she remembered being in a creative writing course with him. And she said, "You know, Joe wrote a really interesting story in that class." She said it was about the funeral of an old politician. The orations are going on about what a great guy he was. But this story is written from the point of view of the wife. And the wife is thinking what a bastard he really was. And my friend said it was interesting at the time that he would write from a woman's point of view. So I thought, there's got to be more to this guy than meets the eye.

Later on, I was with him in Newfoundland for two days, where he was campaigning with John Crosbie for a by-election. And the first question I asked him, as we were flying out, was "What did you notice while you were in Newfoundland?" And he said, "I noticed the little graveyards in the outports, how beautifully they were kept, how they all had little fences around them." I thought that was an interesting observation. He was quite literary, in a sense.

And then I worked it around and said, "I gather you're a fan of Joan Didion's." And we talked about that and I got out of him that really he would have much preferred to be a writer than a politician. That politics was his second choice. And I said, "Why did you give up on the idea of being a writer?" And he said, "Well, it was really when I arrived at the work of that terribly difficult Jesuit poet —" "Gerard Manley Hopkins?" "Yes. That's when I realized I wasn't cut out to be a writer." I saw Clark in a completely different light from those comments. So much of the success of that piece, which I think was one of my best, came from the different perspective I gained about him talking with other people.

One of the principal goals of this type of research is to provide insights that help you look beyond the external impressions that may exist about a person. Joe Clark was seen by the public as "Joe Who," an ineffectual, clumsy politician lacking depth and a chin. Sandra Gwyn encountered a contrary image as she probed his background, dispelling some of the myths prevalent in the media. She was able to approach him, therefore, with a fresh and higher set of expectations.

Often what keeps you from breaking through the surface barrier is the person himself, who may project a public persona as a means of protecting or hiding the real self. When Roy MacGregor was researching an in-depth article on John Turner for the *Toronto Star* during the 1984 Liberal leadership campaign, he kept running into the same old stories, many endorsed by the candidate himself. Most emphasized Turner's ambition and his athletic image as the ladies' man with the blue bedroom eyes. During several phone interviews, however, MacGregor picked up on an unexpected theme:

> One of the great things about being an interviewer is the ability to pretend you know things. It's so wonderful. I was phoning around and this one guy — he was the head of Massey College — said, "John is the type of guy who would sit around in the summer at the cottage and read a book on theology."
>
> So then I phoned someone else and said, "So and so at Massey College was telling me about John reading theology. I understand you know a lot about this interest." And I learned that he might read different versions of the Bible. And then they tell you more things and you pretend more and more with the next person [that you know more than you really do] until finally I had a whole package that had to do with religion.

All that led to me learning, in an interview with him, that he believed in sacrifice. [He believed] that God gave you certain rewards on earth with the idea that you would someday return them even if it cost you. And that's why he's still in there fighting [as Opposition leader]. It's the religion that drives him, not the ambition.

"Knowing how to use one person to get to another is very important," says Jim Dubro. "Once you've found a source, make sure you ask him or her for the names of other people you might contact, and for phone numbers. Then you ask, 'Do you mind if I mention I was talking with you?' That can make a big difference when you call the next person."

Dubro used this ploy effectively during his first contact with ex-mobster Vinnie Teresa. Part of the transcript of their telephone conversation is included in Wade Rowland's book, *Making Connections*. Dubro begins by establishing how he and Teresa have mutual "friends," while pouring on a heavy dose of flattery (which he recommends you do shamelessly):

"I saw Phil Manuel when I was down in Washington." [Manuel is an investigator for the United States Senate's Permanent Subcommittee on Investigations.]

"Oh yeah? He's a good friend of mine." [says Teresa]

"He recommended you quite highly. In fact, he said you were *the* expert on gambling junkets."

"He's right there," says Teresa, "I originated them."

Then Dubro drops another name.

"I was talking to Ted Harrington down in Boston as well. . . ." [Harrington is a U.S. attorney and one of three people mentioned in the acknowledgments of Teresa's book.]

45

And so it went, Dubro using every name he could as common currency. By doing so, he gave the impression, first, that mutual acquaintances had endorsed him, and second, that he knew more than he actually did.

e. WHAT COLOR SOCKS DID YOU WEAR ON YOUR FIRST HEIST?

The magnitude of research required for a book can be mindboggling. In *Murderers and Other People,* a collection of interviews Denis Brian did with renowned interviewers, the author asked writer Gay Talese, "How exhaustively would you interview for a biography?"

> [Right now, I'm doing] a book about gangsters [*Honor Thy Father*] a book about a particular family (the Bonannos). I'm interested in the subject of organized crime in America. I had come to know quite intimately a family: by a family I don't mean in the sense that the Attorney-General identifies families as comprising 400 machine-gun artists. I'm talking about a real family: father, mother, children, grandfathers, uncles, etc. I've come to know a family who in one way or another are on the other side of the law. I've come to know them so well that I am now in a position with veracity to think as they think, which is a lawless way to think.
>
> I have about 700 or 800 interviews. In the case of one person who is a major subject in my book, I have gone through every month of his life — he's 38 years old — I've gone through every month of his conscious life through interviews, from his first year in school as a first-grader, right through his first night in jail, right through his first crime, his first official crime, impressions that he has of his own misdemeanors, felonies, and those who exact judgment over him. I've really covered this man's life through interviews. The son is somewhat around my own age and I know this man very, very well, certainly know him better than his wife does. In many ways I could tell his wife things about him.

During his stint at *Canadian* magazine in the 1970s, Roy MacGregor, who formerly wrote for the *Toronto Star*, learned that "Great writing is great research. The further you go into the research, the more you understand what's really going on in a story. Until then, I would stop researching as soon as I had what I thought was enough material." He recalled the amount of research he carried out for the 1984 profile he did on John Turner during the Liberal Party leadership campaign. "The *Star* gave me about a two-and-a-half month lead time because they presumed, correctly, that Turner would win [the Liberal leadership]," he says. "I ended up with 800 pages of handwritten notes. I interviewed about 60 or 70 people. I had enough there for a book (the profile of Turner that appeared in the *Star* ran about 13,000 words) and when it came out a Canadian publisher immediately offered $25,000 for the rights to a book. Which my agent turned down, saying that we could get $100,000 easily." At this point MacGregor sighs ruefully. Turner was Prime Minister for only a few months before losing a landslide election to Conservative Brian Mulroney, and there was no longer any interest in publishing his biography.

Although generally there is less requirement for such exacting research in the electronic media, some projects —especially investigative documentaries — can demand total immersion in a subject. The purpose of such intensive research is to turn the generalist interviewer into an expert on the subject of the story.

For his investigation of Canadair, the federal corporation that was found to have wasted more than a billion dollars of the public purse on the development of executive jets no one would buy, *the fifth estate*'s Eric Malling submerged himself in a quagmire of research. "For about six weeks, three of us were in here 12 hours a day, on the phone, reading journals and finding on-the-record reports from MOT [the Canadian Ministry of Transport] and the FAA [the American Federal Aviation Association]. We had to learn how to be aviation experts in order to understand a very closed, complicated kind of world. Only then could we interview people with any confidence or authority."

f. CAVEAT RESEARCHER

A note of caution has to be added to this enthusiastic endorsement of research. For the writer, one of the attractions of researching endlessly is that as long as you're researching, you don't have to write. It's a form of procrastination, a way of delaying having to face the tyrannical blank page. But if your article is to be 5,000 words and you gather enough material for a trilogy of books, paring it down can be an overwhelming task. At risk is the possibility that you'll lose sight of your point of view, that the weight and diversity of your material will pull you in too many directions.

For broadcasters, the problem manifests itself on-air. If you are too well briefed, especially on a complex subject, there's a temptation to speak with the guest at too technical or advanced a level. The audience is forgotten, and many of the simpler questions, which are often the most important and hardest to answer, go unasked.

There is also a danger that you start to imagine yourself an expert and become unreceptive to arguments that differ from your own. Jim Reed is a hardnosed interviewer with CTV's investigative program *W5*. A persistent questioner with the wiles of a courtroom lawyer, he relies heavily on thorough research. Nevertheless, he is aware of its pitfalls:

> Too much research can be a handicap. You can be at loggerheads with the interviewee because you have a preset point of view based on what may not necessarily be totally accurate information. One of the things I've discovered over the years is that so much of what . . . comes from newspaper articles and magazine articles is inaccurate. It's like police files. They have so much information on people but so much of it is hearsay or gossip and may not be accurate at all.

g. RESEARCHING FOR RADIO AND TV

My first job in journalism, in 1973, was researcher for the CBC Radio morning public affairs program in Ottawa. It was a three-hour information package that featured no music except for jarring little bursts of instrumental filler to bridge the moments between interviews, editorials, news, weather, and sports. A daily program such as this one or CTV's *Canada AM* is a gluttonous beast, devouring information with a bottomless stomach.

My responsibilities were to line up five or six live or taped interviews a day, type the research on a background sheet, and write a pithy introduction and some suggested questions for the host. Considering that for every story successfully arranged, there were two or three that didn't pan out, it was not unusual to be working on more than ten different stories a day.

Needless to say, I have great sympathy for anyone who does daily research. The workload can grind body and soul into numbing submission.

Nevertheless, despite being gruelling, it's great training. Researchers must become adept at interviewing and producing items in order to survive. They have to select an angle for a story; track down a suitable guest; pre-interview the person; decide on the best format to present the story on-air; and persuade the guest to do the interview, a challenge that is sometimes akin to coaxing a reluctant patient into the dentist's chair.

Almost all the work is done on the telephone, with most stories originating from newspaper articles. The following step-by-step techniques are applicable to all areas of research, but they are of particular relevance to broadcasting:

(a) Have some idea of the story before you start to make calls. Too often researchers pick up the telephone and start talking to prospective guests without knowing what to ask. By doing so, you run the risk of blowing the interview, for you may not get a second chance. This happened to me in my early days as a researcher in a conversation with René Lévesque, the former leader of the Parti Québecois, when he slammed the phone down, cursing me in French and English. My embarrassment taught me a lesson I've never forgotten.

(b) Take a few minutes to read the newspaper clipping, wire copy, or whatever your source is. Then put the clipping aside and figure out the essence of the story. Think of whether and how it could be handled on your program. Consider other potential angles and guests than those in the clipping. Jot down some questions.

(c) Read chapter 3, on getting the interview.

(d) When you make contact with the prospective guest, identify yourself and your program. Make sure you *don't* commit yourself to an interview before speaking with the guest for a while. Don't begin by saying, "We'd like to interview you on such and such a show," unless you know ahead of time the guest is a good speaker and the correct person for the story. Say instead, "I'm doing some research on cancerous tumors in fish (or whatever the topic is), and I wonder if I could speak with you?"

(e) Ask the guest if the original source is correct. Don't assume a newspaper article or wire clipping is accurate or conclusive. Check all names, titles, dates, etc. Don't be married to the source. Use it only as a starting point. On the other hand, just because a guest denies or contradicts what's in an article, don't take the denial as gospel. Take it as an indication that you have to look at the story very carefully. To get a balanced perspective, you may have to call the reporter who originated the piece.

(f) Explore the story with the guest, making sure you really understand what it's about. This may have to be done slowly; and you'll often feel a pressure, from the interviewee, to go through it quickly. Unless you resist that pressure, you'll run into trouble. With a complex subject (or a confusing speaker), this could mean a long and exasperating conversation. You must be confident enough to say, "I'm sorry, I don't understand," until you reach a point of understanding.

As you discuss the story, be alert for angles and information not covered in the source. Be a reporter, not just someone verifying that a newspaper story is accurate.

(g) Make sure you line up the appropriate guest for your angle. When a deadline is looming, there's a great temptation to book anyone who sounds as if he or she will agree to talk. It requires discipline to ensure that you don't cajole or flatter the wrong person just to fill the "hole" (the time allotted in the program for an interview).

Bureaucrats are often asked to comment on policy matters that should really be directed toward a politician. A researcher on a program I produced once lined up the administrator responsible for snow removal in Ottawa. We'd received complaints that sidewalks weren't being cleared as frequently as in the past. "Several senior citizens have phoned us to complain," our host said in his best *j'accuse* voice. "Can you give an explanation for this dangerous situation?" The nonplussed administrator said, "Well, why don't you ask city council? They cut back on our budget. I agree with you and I'd love to have more money. I've been getting the same complaints and I don't like it either." Thud. A one-question interview with the wrong, but crafty, guest.

(h) If the first person you call doesn't seem right, ask him or her to suggest names of other possible guests. Get phone numbers (business and home), and ask which one is the best speaker.

(i) Listen closely to how the person tells the story. If you are gnawing the phone with boredom, this may not be the perfect guest. Is there too much jargon? How does the guest respond when you ask for a translation into layperson's language? Is the guest defensive, hostile, monosyllabic, longwinded, or unable to present information in a logical order? Is there an accent? How thick is it? (Remember it will tend to get thicker under pressure.) Make a note of what questions elicit the best and weakest responses, and which strike nerves, take too long to answer, or produce the liveliest anecdotes.

(j) Unless absolutely necessary, don't use an aggressive tone or style with someone you're trying to book. Your objective is to draw out as much information as possible and then convince the person to repeat it on-air. At the same time, don't misrepresent the intention of the interview — if it's going to involve some tough questions, don't make it sound like it's going to be a sweetheart chat with the host. However, you can ask difficult questions in a friendly way. In other words, don't scare off the guest by trying to be tough when you don't have to.

(k) Before finishing the interview, say, "Is there anything I should have asked that I overlooked?" It's a good habit to develop, because it sometimes opens floodgates of information you would never otherwise have gained.

(l) If the person is not suitable, thank him or her for the time and information. It's important to finish the contact with dignity intact for both parties. Sometimes researchers forget that it's not a crime for someone to be inarticulate or nervous. They can make a person feel devalued because he or she couldn't condense information into a five-minute package.

(m) If the person is suitable, make your pitch. (See chapter 3 for techniques.) Remember that, out of excitement or nervousness, your guest may not hear the details accurately.

Many times in Ottawa, we had guests for CBC Radio turn up at the CBC-TV studios in full makeup and their Sunday best. Go over the logistical details and have your guest repeat them to you. With phone interviews, get all the phone numbers you can. "If you're not there when we call, where else might you be? Is there a back-up number? Here's our studio number where you can call us if there's a problem."

FEATURE INTERVIEW: Leora Aisenberg

Leora Aisenberg is a 25-year-old researcher with CTV's morning public affairs program *Canada AM*. Following completion of the one-year graduate program in journalism at Carleton University, she travelled in Europe for a year and, on her return in 1983, "stumbled into her job" at CTV.

A normal work day for Aisenberg starts at 9:30 a.m. and runs for 10-12 hours, during which time she would book anywhere from one to three items. Like most researchers, she lives on the telephone and has developed a warm but persistent style. Her voice, which has a slight New York-sounding tinge, projects energy and enthusiasm. Our interview was done on the telephone.

PM: Do you think the telephone is a help or a hindrance when lining guests up?

LA: I think it's much better than face-to-face. Especially because I look a lot younger than I am. People who've only met me on the phone are surprised at how young I look when they finally see me. So it makes it easier for me to establish a relationship with them on the phone.

It's also easier to take yourself one step further, to get to know people . . . especially someone who has had something happen to them . . . someone who has been raped, is unemployed. You can talk to someone like that for half-an-hour on the phone and they tend to be a lot more open with you than if I were to say, "Meet you on the corner. . . ."

PM: What do you say to those people?

LA: I usually say two things: one is that we are not putting you on television to exploit you and make you cry; and [the other] is that you have something important to say that could help others, that could be beneficial. [For a story on unemployment, for example] they always say, "I'm so tired of waking up in the morning and seeing these so-called experts talking about people who don't have a job. How would they know?" And if you appeal to that sense — here is your chance to tell people, to tell government, whoever — what it really feels like rather than have somebody else speak for you, I think that helps a lot.

PM: Have you developed a particular style on the phone?

LA: I find self-deprecating humor works, especially in a situation where it is a difficult topic — a complicated business story like the recent Canadian government budget.

53

Obviously, no matter how good a story editor I am, I am not an expert on tax. And I think it's a big mistake to come on the phone and because you feel insecure about the terminology, or whatever areas you are not familiar with, try and fake it. That's the biggest mistake because you always get yourself in trouble.

What happens is that they assume then that you have a sophisticated level of knowledge in this area and they talk up rather than down. And what is going to happen is that they are going to get on the show and because you were the only example of the audience, when they get on the show they're going to talk the same way.

PM: Do you have questions prepared?

LA: I always have questions written out, but half the time I never use them. I'm not concerned about how I sound, I'm more concerned about what I get from this person. Often you have to have research in order to know what to ask. For the budget story, I would have done research before calling a guest. I'd have notes so that if I were in a panic and didn't know what to ask, they're my security blanket.

The notes are also important because often you phone Mr. X, he's out to lunch, so you work on another story and at 2:30 Mr. X phones you back out of the blue. You have to be able to tune yourself right back into that story and the notes help.

PM: Can you give an example of a recent story you worked on?

LA: The Lahr, West Germany one sticks in my mind [the story about Canadian Defense Minister Robert Coates resigning after it was made public that he had visited a bar in West Germany frequented by prostitutes] because when you are doing something in another country it can be really difficult. And that was a situation where every Canadian reporter was on the phone, trying to book this person [the bartender at the club] for that day, before it became an old story.

Speaking to the bartender I had to go from point A, which was, "Please don't hang up on me even though I'm the fifteenth Canadian who has managed to get through to you on the phone today," to point Z, which was, "Please drive two hours to a station in Strasbourg where we will try and set up a satellite and have you live on the show tomorrow." I was literally on the phone with him for over an hour the first time, and he then left the phone line open for me every half-hour from then on. You just have to develop a relationship with somebody like that.

PM: How do you develop that relationship?

LA: First of all by explaining what you want. He's had photographers, reporters trying to get quotes, and mikes put on the phone to get quotes. So I said, I am not quoting you, I am just a person who wants to talk to you. That was the first step.

The second was to say, gee, there's all this controversy here, it's a really big story and you have a major role in it. Does that make you anxious? Is there something you think people will misunderstand? Is there something you have to tell people? So you let the person know that the reason you're talking to him is to get his side of the story, rather than because all of a sudden he's become a celebrity. That can be exciting [for him] but it can also be scary. Especially if you know how he feels when reporters call him up and say, "Your bar is a place for prostitutes." Well, maybe it is and maybe it isn't, but that comes later in the conversation. The first thing you have to establish is, I'm not trying to get that out of you, I'm trying to hear what you have to say first. Once that is established, the person can relax a little and talk to you and you can ask, "Well, listen, how many rooms are there in the back, how many prostitutes go there?" And he won't get his back up right away.

PM: Did he get his back up?

LA: No.

PM: Do you find it hard to unbook (cancel) guests?

LA: Yeah, that's really difficult but it's also important that you handle it well, that you care about how people feel. You hate to lie and I try not to be dishonest with the person because that's not fair. Usually I blame the top news story of the day, which usually is the reason. A more important story has broken and we have no choice but to cover it. People understand this, because that's the nature of the show, to cover breaking stories. I always try to be tactful, though, and to consider their feelings.

3

NEGOTIATING THE INTERVIEW

a. DON'T PRESUME THE AYATOLLAH WON'T TALK

"They ain't said no 'til they've said no." If Yogi Berra had been a journalist, that's what he would have told rookies of the press corps about the attitude required to line up interviews.

In other words, don't presume someone is unwilling to speak until you've asked them. Too many times I've heard researchers or interviewers concede defeat in advance — "There's no way he's going to talk" — then ensure their self-fulfilling prophecy comes true by not even trying. On the contrary, journalistic folklore is replete with tales of "scoop" interviews that often involved no more than picking up the telephone and following through.

If the researcher on the local CBC Radio morning show in Montreal hadn't believed in that credo, *Daybreak* would never have had the first interview with Ayatollah Khomeini following the takeover of the American Embassy in Tehran in November, 1979.

"The day after the takeover, our researcher, Avi Cohen, suggested we try to get an interview with the Ayatollah," remembers Bob McKeown, then the host of *Daybreak* and now a co-host of *the fifth estate*. "This was 6 a.m. in Montreal and we said, 'Sure, Avi,' and thought no more about it.

"Just before 9 a.m. and the end of the program, the red light on the studio phone started flashing and I asked Avi, who was in the control room, who was on the line.

'Guess,' he said, with a triumphant look on his face.

'The Ayatollah?'

'No, but it's someone who speaks English and is sitting beside the Ayatollah.'

"What he had done was to phone Tehran over and over again all morning. You have to go through Paris, which he did 12 times, until he got an operator in Tehran who spoke French. He asked for the Ayatollah's number but it was unlisted. He then called back another 12 times, until he got another French-speaking operator and told her he'd just been doing an interview with the Ayatollah for CBC and had been cut off. If she knew what was good for her and didn't want to invoke the wrath of the leader of the Islamic revolution, she'd better put him back through. This intimidated her enough that she gave him a number to call.

"The number was for a phone on a desk in an area where, under Islamic law, the Ayatollah would meet at a certain time each week to deal with problems and representations from mayors of the various Islamic states. After seven calls to that number, Avi reached a mayor who spoke French and English.

'Would you know what the Ayatollah feels about what's taken place at the embassy?' Avi asked. 'Why don't I ask him?' the mayor replied. 'He's right here.'

"A few minutes later, with the mayor acting as an interpreter, we had the first interview with the Ayatollah after the hostages were taken."

Many of the qualities Cohen displayed — persistence, ingenuity, moxie, and a basic understanding of human nature — are characteristics worth acquiring and refining if you want to learn the art of persuading people to do interviews.

Generally speaking, people like to be interviewed. The oft-quoted observation by the legendary American journalist, A. J. Liebling — "There is almost no circumstance under which an American doesn't like to be interviewed. We are an articulate people, pleased by attention, covetous of being singled out" — is overblown but not far off the mark. North Americans tend to regard media exposure as a sign of status. Appearing on TV or radio or being quoted in print is a form of celebrity, an amplification of Andy Warhol's observation in the 1960s that "everyone will be famous for 15 minutes."

"It never ceases to amaze me how willing people are to be interviewed," says Don Obe, a highly experienced editor and writer. "Not only that, but how willing they are to divulge information to someone who is basically a stranger." That's not to say you're always going to get a "yes" to your request for an interview. Many people, especially those in segments of society often subjected to critical treatment in the media — businesspeople and politicians, for example — perceive a prospective interview as a threat, to be avoided or controlled as much as possible. But even within the most seemingly resistant individuals or groups, there is probably a desire to have their side of the story represented fairly and accurately, which no one else can do better.

b. FEAR OF PHONING

It can be intimidating to pick up the telephone (the means by which the majority of interviews are arranged) and, like a salesperson going into a pitch, try to convince a stranger to grant an interview. A variety of factors may contribute to your reluctance and apprehension. First of all, not everyone is comfortable selling themselves, which, like it or not, is part of the process. Often it's not so much the subject matter that persuades the person but the manner in which the proposal is delivered. A request presented in a shy and nervous manner is more likely to be turned down than one packaged with style, humor, and assertiveness.

Then there's coping with the possibility of rejection, not an enjoyable prospect for anyone. In addition, the potential rejector may be famous, powerful, aggressive, going through terrible emotional stress, under attack publicly, or known to be hostile to the media. It's not without some tightening in the stomach that you call a mother whose child has been killed in a car crash, a politician accused of possession of illegal drugs, or a businesswoman known to equate journalists with lepers and crooks.

If you have trepidations about approaching someone, it could emerge in several subtle but destructive ways. You may be so nervous and passive that you invite the interviewee or media contact to turn you down. Or, if you get the green light, you'll be so grateful to have cleared that hurdle that you'll accept conditions that limit the interview or render it useless. Conversely, you may come on so aggressively — a form of overcompensation — that you offend or scare off the potential guest or media contact.

While these feelings may never go away completely, they can be diminished, partly through experience and partly through just acknowledging they exist. Acknowledging the feelings makes it possible to adjust and compensate for their effect (although just the fact of having admitted your fear usually makes it easier to cope with). If you find it too difficult to "hustle" and sell the interview, you may need to develop a strategy that you're more comfortable with. For example, in situations where time permits, you could initiate a request by sending a detailed outline of your proposal, then following up with a phone call.

For most people, the biggest obstacle to overcome is making the initial move, a problem that doesn't seem to go away with time. "I still find the hardest thing about doing any story is that first phone call," says Roy MacGregor. "But once I get rolling, it begins to fall into place, with one source leading to another."

c. TRACKING DOWN SOURCES

"How can I find this guy?" a student asked me last year, holding up a newspaper clipping with a name underlined. "I want to interview him over the phone and I don't know where he works."

The single greatest resource for any journalist trying to locate someone is the telephone book. It's the first place to look. And don't presume the number isn't listed.

If you don't find the number immediately, don't give up until every conceivable avenue has been explored. For example, if the person is married, the number may be listed under the spouse's first name (if they both have the same surname). Or, if it's an unusual name, you might track the number down by calling others with the same surname, in hopes that you'll connect with a relative.

If you draw a blank with the public telephone directory, there are other sources and routes to explore.

(a) Various city directories list residents by address and telephone number. These are available in all larger libraries. *Might's,* for example, gives addresses and telephone numbers for Toronto by alphabetical street listing. If you know where someone lives but don't have the phone number, you can call neighbors to see if they know the number and will give it to you. If you know a telephone number but not the address, the *Bower's* directory lists numbers numerically, along with the names and addresses. A quicker method, according to an unnamed source in *Finding Canadian Facts Fast*, is to call the local telephone company. "The company itself and police forces use special numbers to trace people. If you can get such a number you can use the service, although it's not officially a public service. By giving the phone number you've traced, you can get the exact address and correct spelling of a name, no questions asked."

(b) Government phone books list employees alphabetically and by department. These can also be found in libraries. In Ottawa and Washington, D.C. the odds of someone working in the government are so high it's often the best place to start, if you want to reach someone during the day.

(c) If you need the number of a public figure, it's worth giving a fellow journalist a call. Although they tend to be covetous of their black books, journalists will often help out a fellow worker, provided you're not with a directly competing outfit. Be prepared, however, to prove who you are. It's not unreasonable for verifiable identification to be demanded.

(d) Names and phone numbers for journalists and other sources on a broad range of issues are available to members of the Centre for Investigative Journalism (CIJ) in Canada, or the Investigative Reporters and Editors (IRE) in the United States. The annual fees for the CIJ are modest ($30 for students, $45 for journalists) and the eligibility requirements fairly loose.

(e) If you're looking for people to speak about a specific subject — epilepsy, illiteracy, native rights, advertising — contact an organization that represents the particular issue. There seems to be at least one organized group for every cause, problem, disease, activity, or inequality you can imagine. These organizations can nearly always be found in the telephone book, if you learn to read it with a researcher's mind. If the subject is artichokes, try such variations as The Artichoke Association of Canada (or its provincial equivalent); The Canadian Association of/for Artichokes; The Association of/for Artichokes Canada; etc. The possibilities are endless. If you can't find an organization, telephone an artichoke producer or anyone who deals with the vegetable and ask who speaks for artichokes in the country.

(f) If you don't want an official spokesperson to interview, ask the contact to help you locate the kind of guest you need. For sensitive issues — a story about how someone copes with a disability, for example —an intermediary can be invaluable in lining up a firsthand source. He or she can screen potential guests to find a person with the disability who is reasonably articulate and willing to participate. Worth remembering, of course, is that you will likely be connected with someone who will represent the particular organization in a positive light.

(g) Don't forget your friends. Whenever you're looking for interviewees — especially for behavioral or relationship issues — ask your friends if they know anyone who'd be suitable. Please note, however, that this approach can have its drawbacks. Since journalists are inclined to associate with like-minded people, certain (usually trendy) types seem to be overrepresented in the media.

When Bob McKeown and Robert Harris were preparing a documentary on Muhammad Ali in 1979, for CBC Radio, "The Greatest" proved to be as elusive to pin down for an interview as he was to catch in the ring.

They followed him from New York to New Orleans, to Miami and Las Vegas, never able to penetrate the phalanx of guards and hangers-on who crowded around him. With the deadline looming, they had all but given up. Their only hope was a man named Harold Conrad, who had befriended them, and was one of Ali's most trusted inner circle.

A former boxing reporter for the *Brooklyn Eagle* and the promoter of one of Ali's first fights, Conrad was revered by Ali because he supported Ali totally when Ali was stripped of his title after refusing to be drafted for the Vietnam War.

Conrad gave them Ali's unlisted number in Chicago and prescribed the following: "Tell him I told you to call. Call him 'the Champ.' He likes to be called 'the Champ.' (At this point Ali had lost his title to Leon Spinks.) Tell him you're from the Canadian government. He likes governments."

At a suggested time, McKeown phoned and a refined female voice answered, "The Ali residence."

"Hello. Bob McKeown from the Canadian *Government* Broadcasting Corporation calling. Harold Conrad arranged for me to call the Champ. Is the Champ there?"

About 30 seconds later, there was a barely audible grunt from the other end of the line. "Hello Champ?" Another grunt. "Champ, I'm from the Canadian *Government* Broadcasting Corporation. Harold Conrad arranged for me to call. We're preparing a documentary on you and we'd like to come and do an interview."

There was about a minute of abject silence. "Uh ... how much you gettin' for this? How much are you payin' me? If you talk to my lawyers and agents, they know how much I'm worth."

"Listen Champ. If you knew how little we're getting for this you'd be utterly embarrassed," McKeown replied honestly. That seemed to disarm the mumbling voice. "We can't afford to pay you anything," McKeown continued, "because we're not making anything ourselves. It's a labor of love."

With that declaration, Ali's tone changed abruptly. The interview was arranged for the next day. And he gave McKeown and Harris directions to give the taxi driver at the airport so they wouldn't be overcharged.

When they arrived the next day, Ali had forgotten about the conversation but welcomed them in. Five hours and a long rambling interview later, they reluctantly declined an invitation to dinner because they had to fly back to Ottawa for work the next day.

d. JUST PHONE AND SAY PLEASE

Most interviews are arranged in one of three ways: by telephone, by letter, or through the intervention of a third party. An interesting exception was the *Playboy* interview with José Napoleon Duarte, the President of El Salvador. Before it could take place, the El Salvadorean cabinet held a special session to debate the merits of granting the interview.

The first step is to choose the method of approach. From my own experience, most interviews are arranged by telephone, especially if you're working on a daily deadline. But the value and impact of a well-written letter should not be underestimated.

I begin with a phone call because it's faster and affords the opportunity to establish personal contact, either with the targeted guest or the person designated to handle media inquiries. If I run into a barrage of flak, I quickly ask if there's a preferred way to present my request. Occasionally the response is yes — "Could you send us something in writing, an outline of what you want to talk about, examples of your work, and a list of questions" — and it's up to me if I want to comply.

For requests made by phone, several basic points should be considered:

(a) Be aware of your telephone style, and work constantly to refine it. If you're obnoxious, submissive, or incoherent, you could easily blow an interview that otherwise would have been agreed to. Bear in mind what CTV's Roger Smith calls the "three Ps": preparation, politeness, persistence.

(b) Tact, natural charm, and sweet talk will almost always get you further than bullying. Knowing when to growl is important, but I always consider it a last resort. Humor helps to diffuse any aggravation caused by your insistence or repeated calls.

(c) Don't pick up the phone until you're clear about the purpose of the interview. I've seen researchers rush to the phone, get right through to an important guest, then not be able to explain just what it is they want. It's only natural for the interviewee to expect some explanation, general or detailed, about your intentions.

(d) Learn who to call. My first few days as a researcher in Ottawa were very frustrating because none of my messages to cabinet ministers were being returned. I quickly discovered there was a protocol to follow, and that certain types of people have to be contacted through a secretary, assistant, or media officer.

Since that time, unless I'm familiar with the protocol, I always ask, "Who should I speak to to arrange for an interview with Mr. Mandarin?"

(e) Unless there is a very good reason for deception, always begin by stating your name, the media outlet you work for, and the reason you're calling.

(f) If you have to negotiate through an intermediary, such as a secretary or media relations person, initiate as friendly a relationship as possible. Remember that this person may be besieged by calls, especially if there's a major story breaking. If your publication or program doesn't have enough clout to guarantee you priority treatment, your style may be the only advantage you have.

Engage the person in a conversation, reducing as many formal barriers as you can. It stands to reason that if he or she warms to you, the chances of success are far greater. If this person has a pile of messages from journalists and knows the boss only has time to return a few, your brief relationship on the telephone could make the difference in having your call returned.

(g) Obtain some commitment as to when you'll receive a return call. If the answer is "by late this afternoon," nail down a time when you can call back to find out. This gives you "permission" to nag. "Hi, I'm calling back to see if the interview is confirmed yet. I'm sorry to bother you, but I also know how busy you must be handling all the requests." If there is no answer at that time, establish another deadline.

(h) If politeness is getting you nothing but polite denials, you may have to turn up the burners and apply some pressure. It's not my style, but some people like to yell and scream. However, I don't recommend it; better to change your tone of voice, displaying your irritation or frustration. And if you feel you're being given the run-around, say so. Pressure can be applied without it becoming a brawl. What's important is to ensure that the final door — getting the interview — doesn't close in your face until all maneuvers have been executed.

A standard and useful line is, "Look, I have to do this story with or without the help of your boss. People accuse the media of not looking at two sides of an issue, but how can we do that if someone won't talk? I can tell you honestly, it's to the benefit of the person involved to present his (or her) side of the story. There's a far greater chance of it being accurate."

Striking a few guilt chords sometimes works. "Look, you gave me the impression I'd have an interview. I told my editor/producer and now my ass is on the line. You can't play games with me like that. All I need is a few minutes (one of the great lines in journalism) — surely you can squeeze that in."

(i) Many media officers are former journalists. They tend to be one of two types: those who turn against the profession with incredible anger and cynicism (they're the hardest to deal with); and those who think they've sold out by leaving the noble trenches of journalism for the plush government and corporate boardrooms. Don't lord it over them with a "you're-just-a-lowly-flack" tone. If you demonstrate some respect and understanding for their position, they will find it easier to remember what it was like being at your end of the phone.

(j) There are times when you have to circumvent the palace guards and find a way to contact your guest directly.

Not all messages are passed along, for some secretaries/assistants take it upon themselves to act as guardians and censors of their beleaguered bosses.

You may have to visit an office or home personally, and be prepared to wait until the person you wish to contact shows up or agrees to see you. It may take a letter, registered or hand-delivered, stating that you want to make sure your request was received and passed along accurately. Or you may have to go through an intermediary.

(k) Nothing is more frustrating than the proverbial "I'm afraid he's in a meeting" response. Invariably, the meeting is open-ended, due to finish sometime between the present and infinity. When encountering this obstacle, explore some possibilities before hanging up:

"Do you know when it's supposed to end?"

"Could be soon," the secretary may reply. "Could be late in the day."

"Could you check his appointment book to see if there's anything else scheduled? That might give an indication of when the meeting has to be over. You see, I have a deadline hanging over me like the Sword of Damocles. If I at least know whether there's a chance for the interview, then I can keep my editor/producer informed."

Another tactic has proven helpful many times. "I just need to speak to her for a few minutes. Would it be possible to get a note taken in to the meeting? Maybe she could call me during a break or at lunchtime."

e. THE PEN IS SLOWER THAN THE PHONE, BUT THE TORTOISE DID BEAT THE HARE

In this day of quick telephone calls and instant communication, a well-written letter still packs a powerful wallop. Think of your own reaction to a ringing phone compared to how you feel about receiving a personal letter in the mail. There can be far more mystery, excitement, and intimacy in a thoughtfully-crafted note than in a routine phone call.

A letter offers several advantages:

(a) It can get you access to certain people who would be difficult, if not impossible to reach by phone. Lisa Howard of ABC was able to get an interview with Fidel Castro by sending him a letter, along with the transcript of an interview she had done with Nikita Khruschev.

(b) A letter has a greater impact than a phone call; it almost demands a reply. Whereas a secretary or media officer might not think twice about ignoring a telephone message intended for their superior, they would be ill-advised to keep a letter from someone it was addressed to. It may be the only way to skirt the media guard and get your pitch directly to the person you want to interview.

(c) Sending letters can be a more gentle means of harassment than a constant slew of phone calls. John Keyes of *TV Guide* (Canada) sent letters on a regular basis for 19 months to the publicist for actor Tom Selleck. As prolonged as the ordeal was, it resulted in Keyes getting one of only three authorized print interviews with Selleck in 1983, no small achievement for a Canadian publication during the rush of Selleck mania at that time.

(d) A letter allows you to control the tone and content of your proposal. Ideas and arguments can be presented unhurriedly and without interference. This is not always the case on the telephone, where your nervousness or the attitude of the person on the other end can affect how the idea is explained and received.

(e) You can include samples of your work, as Lisa Howard did, if you feel it might sway the person's decision. This is most beneficial if you're not well-known, or if the person is suspicious of the media.

You don't always get a positive response. For this book, I wrote to former Prime Minister Pierre Elliott Trudeau, asking if I could interview him about his views on the media. I had read in the paper that he'd joined a law firm in Montreal, and sent my letter there. I outlined the nature of the book, alluded to his well-known disdain for the media, and suggested it would be a chance to have his views exposed to a wide audience, particularly young journalists. Here was an opportunity, I suggested, to influence journalists' practice of their trade.

Knowing full well his reluctance to be interviewed, I offered him an alternative. My preference, I stated, was to speak with him in person or over the phone. But if that wasn't acceptable, I included a blank tape cassette and a list of questions. If he so chose, he could record his responses to those, or address any other points he wished to raise.

About two weeks later a reply came in the mail. "I would like to thank you for your invitation," he wrote. "However, since my retirement from public life, I have been enjoying a 'sabbatical' (his quotation marks) and must, regretfully, decline your kind offer."

Enlisting the assistance of a trusted third party may be an entree to a seemingly inaccessible person. A personal reference still commands a great deal of influence. Many doors are opened in society by taking advantage of mutual contacts. If you can speak to someone who has the ear of the person you're interested in meeting, you increase greatly the chances of an agreement being made.

The intermediary doesn't even have to be a close acquaintance of yours. Sometimes you can use one person to meet another, with that person acting as the negotiator. A rule I find invaluable is to never underestimate the power of even the most tenuous connection.

Jim Reed of *W5* used such a procedure in 1972 to get an interview with Salvador Allende, the President of Chile. Fluent in Spanish, Reed was stationed in South America for CTV:

> I had wanted to interview Allende for quite some time. I had lived in Chile, I knew his background, the background of the government, his personality and his vulnerability. He was a very egotistical man. He was very big on symbolism. But he refused for a long time to do the interview.
>
> So I arranged, through a mutual friend, to meet his wife at a reception. I persuaded her to put my case to her husband. My proposal was to talk about the importance of the President of Chile as a symbol for Latin America and what was happening there. I guess he liked that. He brought his wife to the interview and made a big thing about embracing her and saying how

important the family was in South America. But I knew this was bullshit because he was an incredible womanizer.

It was a violent interview, very argumentative. A crucial moment was when I brought up that, in one of the poorest sections of the city, he had erected a monument to a general who had supported him. This was a *barrio* in Santiago where there was no running water, no school, no clinic, and no sewage system. I asked how he could expect people to support him in the long term when he put more emphasis on this monument than on services to the people.

He got very upset and talked about the importance of symbols. And then he got on a real roll and said how he knew there were 350 CIA agents operating in Chile and trying to undermine his government. He said I didn't understand Latin America, the mentality. He saw me as just an arrogant, slightly overbearing *gringo* from North America who was trying to tell him that he was doing wrong.

But by provoking him with the symbolism theme, I think he came out and said things he wouldn't otherwise have said, especially about the CIA. It was a good example of how to get an interview and the benefit of having a central theme to propose and pursue.

f. I HAVE A RIGHT TO THIS INTERVIEW

Once you reach the prospective interviewee directly, you may still have to go through a teeth-pulling session to convince the person to give an interview, especially for broadcast.

One of the masters of persuasion I observed was an aggressive English woman who worked the telephone like a veteran bill collector. I would listen in admiration and embarrassment as she cajoled or badgered guests to appear on our radio show. More than anyone I've met, she had — or at least projected — a loud and powerful belief that all government, industry, and elected officials had an obligation to speak to the public. She usually used that sanctimonious attitude as a last resort, but it was a deadly ace in the hole.

"This is a public issue and someone has to discuss it," she would say. "If you can't or won't do it, who can you get me that will?" — which laid the problem squarely in the prevaricator's lap. "I can't leave here until I've got another interview, so I must have another name if it's not going to be you." She had the tenacity to wear people out, having learned that if she hung in there, putting the onus on them to solve her problem, most would capitulate under the pressure.

Although I found this woman's style crossed the border too often into the obnoxious, she taught me many things. The most valuable lesson concerned attitude. Through the sheer force of her conviction that she had a right to ask questions and request interviews, she accomplished many of her objectives. I soon learned that that same power could be exerted quietly and with dignity, which suited my nature better. The key was believing in my purposes. I found that when I really didn't believe I had "a right to know," I could hear it in my voice. That helped me decide when to press and when to back off.

I really don't think you can persuade people to act against their will. Leverage can be applied and vulnerabilities played upon, but the bottom line is, if they say yes it's because they want to. Whether that's the right decision — or one that you should have coaxed out of them — is another matter.

When lining up interviews, some aspects of human nature are worth bearing in mind:

(a) Many people are afraid of the media (see chapter 4). First of all, it's a form of public speaking, especially for a broadcast interview. Then there's the concern that they'll make fools of themselves, get fired for saying the wrong thing, be misquoted, or be quoted out of context. Don't ignore those fears. Address them head on if you sense they exist. Make sure the purpose of the interview is clear. The more a person is kept in the dark, the more nervous and reluctant he or she is likely to be.

(b) Offer a reason for doing the interview. Lurking inside everyone is the question, "What's in it for me?" Ottawa psychologist Tom O'Hara feels that too often interviewers forget to consider the needs of the people they're dealing with. "As an interviewer, you have goals that you want to accomplish. Well, an interviewee has goals too, and they need to be addressed: for example, how will I come across, what's the right thing to say, how will I benefit if I agree to talk to you, how will you use the interview? These are legitimate concerns and, if you ignore them, it's bound to affect how the person deals with you and how much you get out of him or her."

(c) As mentioned in chapter 2, give them a reason why they should do the interview.

(d) For broadcast, you may have to coax nervous or hard-to-get guests with a combination of reassurance and flattery. When I was a researcher, it was not untypical, after a successful chat about the topic in a rather informal manner, that a seemingly eager guest would get cold feet when the mention of appearing on-air came up. You will quickly learn to recognize when someone actually wants to do the interview but needs some prompting. If a person is adamantly opposed to doing the interview, that attitude will come through loud and clear. In its absence, hang in there.

There will be occasions when the "three Ps" don't produce results, and more creative — sometimes outrageous — methods may have to be employed. Before choosing a course of action, make sure you've examined it carefully. If you opt for derring-do, be clear about what risks — particularly to other people — may ensue. If you're resigned to staying strictly on the straight and narrow, consider that laziness, inhibition, or lack of creativity may lie behind that decision. I don't believe being a journalist gives you carte blanche to disregard whatever laws, rules, or codes of behavior you find in your way. On the other hand, you won't get far sitting back passively and expecting the story to come to you. What's needed is a philosophy that has some perspective.

g. PICKUPS AND OTHER FUN ASSIGNMENTS

"There's nothing more difficult than a pickup," says Diane Francis, business writer with the *Toronto Star*. "That's where you're a cityside reporter and there's been a slaying and you have to go to the grieving family and get a picture of the slain person or the person who jumped off a bridge. This is tough to do because you need a hell of a lot of chutzpah, skill, and salesmanship. I think everybody should have to do it. It's excellent training for tough interviews. I mean, there's nothing [prominent Canadian businessman] Conrad Black could say to me in a heated conversation that would compare with the emotion of doing a pickup."

I'm glad I've never had to do it. My natural inclination is to leave people alone, not intrude at such a private, traumatic time. But pickups have to be done, because pictures and quotes are necessary for stories. If a child is killed at a busy intersection that should have traffic lights, printing a picture and including comments from the family will have a greater impact upon the community than just a few words of copy. That picture might be the impetus needed to have lights installed. But even if there's no such obvious moral value, the simple truth is that a picture and quotes help tell — and sell — the story.

Approaching people when they're undergoing severe emotional stress is not easy. It's a delicate task and one that most of us are ill-prepared for. Journalists are told they're supposed to be hardboiled enough to be able to ring the doorbell of a family whose child has been found murdered and sexually abused, and to ask for a recent photograph and some quotes without "getting involved" or "taking it home."

But how can you *not* be affected? How can you pretend the feeling side of you doesn't exist? If you deny what's happening within you, it may surface as aggression, cynicism, or depression. And it's bound to influence how you cover the story and interact with the protagonists. The solution is not to become a bowl of mush, however. If you dive headfirst into every emotional caldron that comes your way, you can burn out very quickly. Being overly sentimental or too identified with the victim or underdog can produce just as much bad journalism as the heartless approach. You don't do people any favors by trumpeting their cause too loudly. Better to shape the material subtly in the interpretation you believe is accurate.

What it comes down to is establishing a code of behavior that you can live with, based on more than just the loosely defined rules of journalism. Judy Nyman of the *Toronto Star* says that, despite advice from her editors to maintain distance in emotional stories, she can't hide how she's responding:

> You can't interview a bereaved family by phone because they're going to hang up on you. You can't say, "By the way, can I come over?" You just show up. That's one time you don't make an appointment. Fifty percent of the time you're going to get the door slammed in your face, but that's the chance you take.
>
> I always try to think of the situation as one where somebody close to me has died, either my family or somebody I know. I try to relate to it that way. I'll say, "I know it's not a good time. I can't feel what you're going through. I can understand it but I certainly can't pretend to feel it. But you have to understand that, aside from this being my job, people want to know what happened. Maybe it can prevent a similar thing from happening."
>
> Everything to me is personalities. You have to judge it by the person. You see the person and you get a feel for . . . what you can ask and what you can't.

The opposite of Nyman's sensitive touch is illustrated by a situation described in a 1985 NBC program on the media entitled *Warts And All*. One of the incidents the program examined was the coverage of the murder of a middle-aged woman that took place near Seattle. On the evening of the killing, a reporter came out to the trailer home of the woman's grieving daughter.

"First came the murder, then came the media," the daughter recalled. She said the reporter wedged his foot in her front door and tried to force his way in, badly bruising her shoulder in the struggle. "He yelled at me, 'What's the matter with you, lady, I didn't murder anyone!' "

In the same program, *Denver Post* reporter Marjie Lundstrom outlined a positive experience she had interviewing a family whose teenage son had committed suicide.

"I was fairly brief on the phone. I told them I was very sorry about what had happened and that I knew I was interrupting at a time when they were obviously in grief, but that there was a story that I wanted to do here," she said. (This was a situation where an initial telephone call seems to have been the right choice.) "And I outlined basically what I wanted to do — take a look at Sam's death, Sam's life. I said I thought that teen suicide was a very important issue today, and it needed to be talked about. And he [Sam's father] agreed."

Sam's father confirmed that Lundstrom's objective was the reason he said yes. "I said I would consider an interview if she would do it for the benefit of other families, other people." Following publication of the article, both Sam's parents felt they had done the right thing. Phone calls and letters from parents convinced Sam's mother that "it did some good for other families."

You have to be prepared to encounter all kinds of reactions when you interview people who are in shock or under stress. Some will vilify you with an intensity that will be deeply disturbing. Some will threaten or attack. Others, however, will welcome the opportunity to speak to a sympathetic listener. The interview might be beneficial and/or cathartic. In those circumstances, you may be given information that wouldn't come out if the person was in greater control. "I will protect them [in a situation like that]," says author and journalist June Callwood. "I might ask, 'Is that what you want me to say? Are you sure?' You can't take advantage of people just because they're going through some trauma and it makes a better story."

h. THE AMBUSH INTERVIEW

When all avenues of negotiation have failed, there is always the surprise or "ambush" interview. For a print reporter, just showing up at the house or office might succeed. The conversation will likely begin with a reiteration of the refusal, but once you've made the personal contact, you at least have a fighting chance of persuading the person to reconsider. Often the conversation just eases into the areas you need to cover. If you get your foot in the door, literally or figuratively, the biggest obstacle has been overcome.

For broadcast interviews, arriving unexpectedly with a TV crew or radio tape recorder tends to have the opposite result. (With radio, you can at least conceal the recorder until a positive impression has been made on the subject.) When someone is surprised by a combat team of reporter, cameraman and sound person, the situation tends to polarize. There's little time or opportunity for conciliation. What occurs is usually a form of guerrilla theater, with the "target" looking guilty as charged.

The TV ambush became popular during the post-Watergate heyday of "investigative" journalism. It has now fallen considerably out of favor, although it still prevails. One of its main exponents was Geraldo Rivera, the host of ABC's public affairs program *20/20*. But he later reconsidered its fairness and value:

> It's worthless to confront an executive in a parking lot when he's not going to tell you anything anyway, and put that on TV. I used to justify it by saying, "That's proof that we tried everything to get them to play." But it's not really. All it does is make a show out of "watch the target squirm." It adds temperature, but it doesn't add substance. . . .

We should do everything we can to get all sides to participate and that includes, in my opinion, telling them the areas that are going to be covered in the questioning. That includes saying we'll meet you any time, any place. We'll honor any reasonable conditions.

FEATURE INTERVIEW: James Glasgow

James Glasgow is a Canadian writer and broadcaster who has worked as a freelancer for 15 years in Britain and various parts of North America and now resides in London. This interview was done through the mail. I sent him a cassette and several pages of questions.

PM: What do you think of public relations people? Are they a help or a hindrance?

JG: Obviously it depends on the individual, but overall I think they're very useful. They can provide information and do a lot of the boring arrangements. For many interviews now, they're unavoidable. If you want to get to a big star in Hollywood, you have to go through an agent or studio flack. The first thing to do is to find out the right person to contact.

I employ a process of telephone calls and letters. I'll phone first and try to create a kind of relationship, as friendly as possible. Then I'll send a letter to confirm the conversation and add a more formal level. Sometimes it takes months, even years, of doing this to get to someone particularly popular. It depends, too, on what kind of clout your publication or program has.

Where I find PR people a problem is when the interview actually begins. Many of them want to sit with you, which I find interferes with the intimacy I want to establish with the guest. It's like having your parents in the room while you're trying to neck with your girlfriend. It's hard to be passionate. There was a PR person present when I interviewed Victoria Principal. But after a few minutes of listening to her talk, I felt it wouldn't have mattered if the Holy Trinity had been sitting in. She didn't have much to say.

The PR types will also tell you, "Whatever you do, don't mention the divorce/drugs/face lift," whatever. These, of course, are exactly the things I want to raise. I usually nod in agreement, sort of mumbling so it sounds as if I've agreed. But in truth I've said nothing but "hmphh," which you can't be held accountable for. I find the guests are nearly always willing to talk about these subjects as long as you bring them up judiciously. I remember Nana Mouskouri's flack telling me not to mention her recent divorce or she'd walk out of the interview. Well, I gently eased toward the subject, a little warily, only to have Nana bring it up herself. And she went on and on about it well past the time I wanted to spend on it. It was therapeutic for her.

PM: You've interviewed a lot of business people. Are they difficult to get access to?

JG: Very much so. People don't realize that the CEO [Chief Executive Officer] of a large corporation or bank is virtually in the superstar status. He's like a Wayne Gretzky. His time is extremely valuable and not to be wasted.

Unless I have a previous connection, I always send a letter before making a call. I write it in a very businesslike fashion, presenting an agenda, objectives, and outlining areas of questions. [I include] as much information as possible, because these people are suspicious of the media. They also have had to deal with a lot of reporters who know nothing about business, and are prejudiced against businesspeople. So I make sure I've done my research and that that is reflected in the letter. Basically what I try to do is approach them as one businessperson to another, because being a freelancer is basically running a small business.

PM: Do you include examples of your work?

JG: Selectively, yes. Because I've written for a lot of business magazines, especially here in the U.K., I have a large enough selection to send something that lets them know what to expect. I think it's often the turning point in getting their cooperation.

I wanted to do a profile of the president of a large manufacturing plant that was branching out to design components for outer space habitation. I had heard that he was far from enamored with the media, one reason being that an article had been done on him that sort of poked fun at the whole outer space concept. So along with a detailed letter I included an article I had done on another company that was trying to develop a rather offbeat product — golf balls with a tracking device inside them so they wouldn't get lost — and a letter I'd received from the president of that company after my article came out. It was very positive, mentioning the beneficial publicity the article had created. This, I was told afterwards, was what swayed the space design manufacturer to speak to me.

PM: What are some of the more unusual methods you've used to get interviews?

JG: I don't think it's that uncommon, but I've placed ads in newspapers. I know that George Plimpton and Jean Stein did this for the book *American Journey: The Times of Robert Kennedy*. They wanted to get the thoughts of people who had stood by the tracks watching the funeral train carrying the senator's body from New York to Washington [D.C.]. They put ads in newspapers and received great responses.

I placed ads in the personal columns of several London papers for a feature I was doing on people involved in long-term adulterous — for want of a better word — relationships. I assured anonymity and was quite pleasantly surprised at the number of responses, from women particularly. They were frustrated at being the "other woman," stuck in love with a guy who wouldn't leave his wife or set them free.

I once sent flowers, along with an interview proposal, to a British actress who had declined my more formal requests. Her secretary sent back a note declining once again and thanking me for the flowers, which had been forwarded to a local hospital.

The most outrageous stunt I know about was done by a friend of mine here in London, Oliver Hampton, who wanted to interview the head of a large American corporation. The man commuted to England on a regular basis. All my friend's requests, through the London office, were turned down. But, in speaking with a secretary many times, he learned that the man wasn't picked up at the airport, that he came in by taxi. Oliver then sweet-talked the woman into giving him details of when he arrived at the airport.

The next time the executive was due in, my friend hired a limousine and went out to the airport. He had the American paged, and introduced himself as a representative of the London office who'd been sent to pick him up as part of a new policy.

When they were far enough into traffic so there was no backing out, he told him the truth and asked for an interview, saying that if the man was offended he'd get out and have the limo take him the rest of the route alone. The executive was taken aback but admired his style. They did the interview on the way into the city.

PM: What's your philosophy about getting interviews?

JG: I believe in the old cliché that you can't win if you don't play. To me, what's important is how you treat people. I believe in my job and my right to ask people for interviews. But I don't have the attitude that it's a divine right. I try to be sensitive and flexible. People can sense that, I believe, and when they do, most of them are willing to cooperate. I try to think of how I'd feel if I were the prospective interviewee. That really helps. I'm persistent, but not obnoxious.

4

THE OTHER SIDE: BEING INTERVIEWED

If interviewing is a skill that can be taught and learned (which I believe it can be, to a certain extent), then the same should apply to being interviewed. Why, I wondered, should only one partner in the tango know the steps? If journalists feel the need to prepare, rehearse, and employ specific techniques for an encounter in which they are in ultimate control (and are more familiar and comfortable with the medium and/or its technology than the guest), does it make sense that the interviewee should go in cold?

In the last few years I have conducted media training seminars, primarily with middle management officials in the federal government. I started offering this service because of my experience as an interviewer in Ottawa, when I came across many government representatives who were clearly terrified and unsure of what to do when speaking with a journalist. Too often I would approach an interview with great anticipation — knowing the topic was interesting and deserving of public attention — only to come away frustrated because the person designated to explain the issue was paranoid, incapable of putting thoughts into everyday language, or otherwise inarticulate for reasons that went beyond natural shyness or nervousness.

"People won't be natural if they start worrying about more than just answering the questions," a colleague said to me. "They'll just use the information you give them to become more smooth and sneaky, to manipulate and distort more than they already do." I gave this point great thought, because I wondered if somehow I would be "selling out to the enemy" if I divulged any trade secrets. In reply, I said, "How 'natural' is an interview? Don't we use our information, preparation, and understanding of the process to help us achieve some very specific and planned objectives? Don't we work at the mechanics of the interview to free us to be spontaneous? Sure, some interviewees will take the information and use it to become better, or maybe just more obvious, manipulators. But there are interviewers who do the same. I'm convinced that, for many interviewees, a major part of their difficulty is in not knowing the rules of the game, and that fear of the unknown — not understanding what an interview is really about — is the source of much of their paranoia and unwillingness to provide information."

In the five years since, my conviction has only been strengthened. Being interviewed is a skill, one that can be learned and improved upon with knowledge and practice. I believe most people, by understanding more clearly what is required and expected of them, tend to be more relaxed, concise, and entertaining — in short, they become better communicators. That usually works to the benefit of both the journalist and the interviewee.

It's not all rosy, mind you. Some do indeed become better schmooze artists, able to evade questions with greater ease. I've seen no evidence, however, to indicate they were any more forthcoming with information *before* acquiring a few communication skills. They were just clumsier at how they went about it. To some extent, their glibness just exposes their prevarications — "he's too smooth to be true" — in another way.

A different "drawback" resulting from the sharing of information about interviewing — at least from the perspective of some interviewers — is more interesting to examine. With interviewees better prepared to protect and explain themselves, they are not the pushovers they once were, an improvement that not all my colleagues are grateful for. The more you keep someone in the dark, according to this point of view, the greater the advantage you hold over that person.

When the tally sheet is added up, I believe the benefits of sharing the process with potential interviewees far outweigh the risks, if indeed there really are any.

One of the people appalled by the idea of "helping the other side" is Terence McKenna, a documentary-maker with the TV program *The Journal*, who was reluctant to be interviewed for this book. Our meeting had been arranged through the program's publicist, so he went along with it, but his discomfort was pronounced:

> I don't like the idea of talking to you because the information I give you could end up in the wrong hands. There are people out there who will use what you write to learn how to get out of answering questions. There are all sorts of people, including journalists, who are teaching politicians, businessmen, how to be interviewed. I don't want to contribute to that. I also know that people are going to pick up this book and say, this is the way I go about things. And since I'll be doing interviews in this country for the next 30 years, I'm not sure that's a good idea.
>
> I think the interviewee has overwhelming odds. You have to come into his territory. You have to familiarize yourself with a story he knows better than you do. It's hard to get to a level where you can compete with him, which is why a book like this makes me nervous.

Within the intimate and often tense environment of a small seminar group, I've learned an incredible amount about interviewing through my contact with people on the other side of the notebook, microphone, or camera. More than anything, I've rediscovered the responsibility I have as an interviewer to the other human being involved in the process. I've learned that I can't just barrel in, push my weight around, or exploit some trusting, vain, or dim-witted interviewee without considering the moral and ethical consequences. On the other hand, that doesn't mean I stay quiet or passive when the interview calls for an aggressive or strongly adversarial approach. What it does mean is that I strive to be conscious of my behavior, so that my words and actions are not chosen indiscriminately. The result is a heightened awareness of how the guest is responding to me, which is essential to know, especially for tough interviews.

This deliberate focussing on the guest does not produce a loss of power or any other negative results. On the contrary, I believe it's the key to more successful and disciplined interviewing. Rather than hiding behind pseudo-aggressive techniques, such as intimidation or manipulation, it allows you to direct your energy towards listening and understanding what's happening with the guest and you. The emphasis shifts from playing games and getting hung up on whether you "won" or "lost" the interview, to subtler yet more elusive goals, such as trying to get the right information, or finding ways to release a guest from as many unnecessary pressures as possible so that the information can come out.

In his autobiography, *Donahue: My Own Story*, TV interviewer Phil Donahue looked back, with some self-criticism, on how he and fellow journalists had responded to the needs of people they'd interviewed during times of great stress:

> In Dayton [Ohio] we once covered a tornado and interviewed people still in shock, some of them with house insulation still in their hair. In the background, the viewer saw the place where the house had once stood, a pile of splinters. We would rush the dramatic footage ("It sounded like a train. I thought we were all dead.") to the lab, edit and bang out the script for a bulletin and then the longer, more detailed story for the evening newscast. Then we'd all go out for a beer and glory in the fact that we had beaten the competition by eight minutes, order more beer and go over the "great footage" we had. "Did you see the bike hanging from the tree?" The fact that scores of people that night went homeless or had lost all their property (if not their loved ones) never occurred to us.

a. LOVING AND LOATHING

There is an inherent contradiction in how the public responds to the media that never fails to baffle me. On the one hand, there seems to be an intensive and ever-growing fear and distrust of journalism. A *Time* magazine poll in 1983 showed public confidence in the press to be 13.7% (12.7 for TV), compared to 29% in 1976. In that same poll, U.S. government bureaucrats had the confidence of 13.3% of the respondents. Thus, seen from the outside, the accused and accuser were regarded with equal disillusionment.

On the other hand, most people are eager to cooperate with the media by answering questions or going along with whatever media event is being staged. My unscientific assessment is that the majority, if asked to provide information or comment on the record, are still willing to take part. Not only that, many do it with style. "I'm struck at how good people are at being interviewed," says political reporter Richard Gwyn. "It's because they watch interviews on television, hear them on radio, hour after hour, every day. We're a nation of interviewees. We're training them every day."

Just how powerful that training can be is underlined in the disturbing results of an experiment related by Donna Woolfolk Cross in *Mediaspeak:*

> Offered a chance to "be somebody," most people will share with millions things they would hesitate to tell their best friends. A fascinating experiment conducted by novelist Jerzy Kosinski offers startling testimony to this. Kosinski interviewed a group of ten-to-fourteen-year-old school children individually, asking them very personal questions such as "Do you masturbate?" and "Have you ever stolen anything?" Embarrassed, the kids mumbled, hedged and wouldn't answer completely. Kosinski described what he did next:
>
> "I said, 'Now, I'll tell you why I asked you all these questions. You see, I would like to film the interview and show it on television. . . . Your parents, your friends, strangers, the whole country would see it. . . . All the students assured me they were willing to try harder to answer the same questions. . . .

"Once the equipment was installed, I started the video camera and it was time to address my first 'guest.' Now tell me, I asked, . . . 'do you masturbate?' The boy, suddenly poised and blasé, leaned toward me. 'Well, yes, occasionally I do. Of course, I'm not sure I can describe it. But I can try. . . .'

"And the boy described all, leaving nothing to the public's imagination. I changed the subject. I said, 'Everyone will be interested in your experiences as a thief. Have you ever stolen anything?' Pensively, as if recalling a pleasant childhood incident, the boy said, "Every once in a while when I go to the five and ten, you know, I like to pick up something. . . .' " (The Kosinski quote originated in *Remote Control: TV and the Manipulation of American Life*, by Frank Mankiewicz and Joel Swerdlow.)

Most of the other children performed similarly. Kosinski says that in contrast to the first, off-camera interviews, the children were willing — even eager — to talk on-camera "about the most incriminating subjects, ranging from less common sexual experiences to acts of violence, the very betrayal of one's family, friends, etc." He adds, "Often I pretended to be embarrassed by what they said. But trained in the best talk show tradition, the guests were not put off by their host."

This example shows the media to be a powerful magnet, seductively drawing people toward it with promises of instant notoriety. TV is especially appealing, with its large audiences and intimations of stardom, but print has a strong allure as well. When someone is mentioned or featured in a newspaper or magazine article, the chances are very high that the reference will be clipped and saved to commemorate a significant event in the person's life. Many people crave being singled out and publicly identified as having something worthwhile to say, a need that can be taken advantage of if not held in respect by the journalist.

One interviewee's pleasure, however, can be another's poison. For some, being interviewed is akin to torture, a traumatic prospect that fills them with dread. I find it interesting that while it's universally accepted that giving a speech in public is one of the most terrifying ordeals most people can face, there's far less compassion for the nervous interviewee. Although the two experiences aren't identical, there are many similarities, especially between public speaking and being interviewed on radio or television. Actress Tallulah Bankhead, as quoted in *The Art of Interviewing for Radio, Television and Film* by Irv Broughton, describes her extreme fear when she had to give a live talk on radio:

> As I faced the microphone, it assumed the guise of a contraption that might let loose a death ray. I had a feeling such as I experience when an ether cone is slipped over my nose. There is a pounding in my ears, a buzzing in my head. My hands grew frosty. A dank dew coated my brow. My first word sounded like the caw of a crow. Fearful those invisible thousands might not hear me, I shouted. I was reading from a prepared script and my hands shook so violently the words blurred.

I have seen people in a radio studio freeze solid with fear, turning into a block of ice with bulging eyes. When that happens, a broadcast interview can become a Zen experience, as Jim Wright discovered when he did a live interview for CBC Radio's *Morningside* with a petrified author:

> The guest had written a book, a sort of dictionary of slang terms. He was sitting across the table, which was about two feet wide. He wouldn't look at me, he looked away at the corner of the studio the whole time.
>
> I said, "Well, Mr. So-And-So, let's look at some of these terms. What does this mean?"
>
> Silence.
>
> "Well, it says in your book . . ." and I went on to explain what he'd written. "Let's look at another word. Perhaps you can tell us a bit about this one?"

Silence. Not a word.

"Well, it says here . . ." and I talked for about 10 minutes. By the end I was just going through the pages making comments. I might as well have been alone. At the merciful end, he ran out of the studio. He may have grunted a few times during the interview, but I don't remember him having spoken a word.

Fear of that magnitude can have many origins. Journalists sometimes forget that it's not a crime to find the interview process unnerving. Being questioned, particularly by a tough, well-prepared interrogator, can evoke memories of our childhood relationship with our parents or other authority figures. In *The Art of Interviewing for Television, Radio and Film*, author Broughton quotes Jacques Lalanne, President of *L'Institut de Développement Humain*, in Quebec, on this commonly shared apprehension:

It is no surprise that questions make most of us feel uneasy. They remind us of times we'd rather forget. As children, before we learned the smaller skills of excuse and evasion, questions were often a prelude to accusations, advice, blame, orders, etc. At home, we'd be asked what we did or didn't do, and one seemed as bad as the other. At school, most questions seemed designed to ferret out what we didn't know rather than what we did.

Depending on the individual, insecurities of varying degree can surface. A prominent business executive, who sought my advice on how to conquer his overwhelming fear of being interviewed, confided the following story:

Whenever I'm interviewed, I go into a total panic. It feels as if I'm suffocating. My chest tightens, my heart pounds. I have to really struggle to breathe. When the questions come, I lose the poise and articulateness I normally have. Words are hard to find. I babble or hide behind incomprehensible language, which I can hear is nothing but evasive, meaningless garbage.

And it's a vicious circle. The more I do this, the more the interviewer interrupts, applies the pressure. It's a horrible experience.

I first thought it was just nervousness ... but after a while I realized it was associated with how my father spoke to me when I was a child. He would ask me questions in a loud voice, get angry if I didn't respond right away or the way he wanted me to. It got to a point where I could barely speak in his presence. I'd just let him bully me, which is what I see it as now. When I'm being interviewed, especially by an aggressive male — it's easier with a female interviewer — those old feelings come right back up.

Because these feelings are common, journalists are not exempt from bouts of fear or paranoia when the tables are turned and they become interviewees. In fact, having written articles about the media, I've found they are as thin-skinned, paranoid, and uncooperative as any group — perhaps more so, because they know only too well the tricks of the trade.

A freelance magazine writer who I interviewed for this book found the experience totally disconcerting, even though he tape-records most of the interviews he conducts. "This is very intimidating," he said, staring at my tape recorder. Several times he went to turn it off after a difficult question had been posed, an unacceptable action once an interview has begun. "I'm amazed that people stand up to it as well as they do," he concluded when the ordeal, as he described it, was over.

What these points illustrate is a simple, human fact: fear of being questioned or concern about how you'll be represented is not uncommon, nor is it indicative of more sinister motives, unless there's evidence to the contrary.

b. CASE HISTORY: THE BUREAUCRAT AND THE STARSTRUCK FLY

"The media are pigs, they're disgusting, they're all animals of the lowest form. You just get burned if you deal with them," a nervous young government bureaucrat said bitterly to his fellow participants at a media workshop I conducted in 1981. His outburst, which lasted for several minutes, was unpleasant but a welcome relief. I had felt his hostility from the outset but had chosen not to confront it. This attack, triggered by some casual remark, provided an opening. I coaxed the following story out of him:

> I received a call one Friday from a person at *Canada AM* asking me to come on the program Monday morning to discuss a new study we'd done on farming. It was a controversial report, and I advised the person that I could only talk about the content of the study, how it was done, what the conclusions were. Under no circumstances could I, as a bureaucrat, comment on what policy implications it might have. I told her questions of that type should be put to a politician. She assured me that was understood.

> I then informed the office of the department head about the interview and his assistant told me to get out of it, that it was too risky. He was afraid I'd be put in a position where I'd be asked my opinion. So I called the program back, but they said it was too late to back out. They really squeezed my arm. So I agreed to it. When I reported back to the assistant, he said, "Just remember one thing: in our eyes you can only lose on this."

> I couldn't sleep Sunday evening. I tossed and turned and kept on imagining all sorts of awful things happening. I'd never been interviewed before, so I would have been nervous anyway. But this was terror.

> When I got to the station the next morning, at some ungodly hour, they put me in a studio by myself, with just a camera in there pointing at me. They hadn't told me the interviewer would be in Toronto and I wouldn't see the person, I'd just have a voice coming through an ear mike. So there I sat, hot lights, sweat pouring off me.

And you can guess what happened. The first question this disembodied voice from Toronto asked was about policy. I panicked, literally. And as I struggled — probably more like squirmed — trying to think of what to say, how I was going to keep my job, a fly landed on the tip of my nose! It must have been hovering in the studio, waiting for me. I thought afterwards that they released them deliberately, put honey in my makeup to get them to land on my face. Well, that did it. I froze. I didn't know what to say, what to do about the fly. They asked another question. I mumbled something. This went on for a couple of minutes before it was finally over.

I was humiliated. They had lied to me and set me up. I vowed then and there never to trust the media again.

This incident brings to light several interesting points. Foremost is the unclear communication between the two parties. Lacking either the information or sensitivity to each other's needs, they set a disastrous interview in motion. It could have been avoided.

When the program's researcher telephoned the bureaucrat, she should have realized he was the wrong guest. First of all, he made it clear he wouldn't express any opinions, a deadly restriction for a controversial topic. Second, he was too far down the pecking order to have opinions worth eliciting. He wasn't responsible for or involved in any of the policy decisions. When you add his nervousness — which must have been apparent over the phone — and his attempt to cancel after the fact, you have to wonder about the researcher's judgment.

My conjecture — based on my own experience, in which I lined up guests for the wrong reasons — is that the researcher was desperate for an interview and late on a Friday afternoon, saw the bureaucrat as nothing more than a warm body to fill an empty space in the lineup. Perhaps she thought he was lying when he said he couldn't comment beyond the facts, figuring that once on-air he would have to come across with more substance than he was providing over the phone. Perhaps his contempt for the media came through and, deliberately or unconsciously, she decided that he deserved whatever rough treatment awaited him in the interview. Or perhaps there was a more venal motive, such as wanting to get home at a decent hour. Whatever the reason, and it could have been a combination of several factors, she chose to ignore loud alarm signals warning her to bail out. And as any researcher knows, when those are disregarded, trouble awaits.

But the bureaucrat was also at fault. When I spoke with him, it became apparent that he hadn't clearly explained to the researcher the exact limitations he was bound by or why they were imposed. He assumed she knew how the hierarchy of the government worked. Nor did he suggest any alternatives, such as the name of a more senior person to contact. Instead, he agreed to an interview that he knew beforehand would be a tragedy. And when he called back to cancel, he hadn't the gumption to hold his ground. Instead, he capitulated and spent the weekend in a panic, imagining the worst. Not surprisingly, when you expect calamity, it tends to hit you right on the nose.

Nevertheless, the responsibility for this disaster lies primarily with the researcher. My own observation from my media training seminars is that people who are unskilled with the media can be bullied with surprising, often pathetic, ease. The end result, however, may be a paper victory. But unless you have the goods and put the questions to the right person, all else is nothing but wind and noise.

c. WHAT'S AT STAKE
Directly connected to people's apprehension about being interviewed is a justified or imagined concern about the consequences of their remarks. "I don't think some journalists really understand that people just can't tell them everything without thinking about the impact of their public statements beyond the needs of the reporter," says

Sam Hughes, the former President of the Canadian Chamber of Commerce. "They seem irritated if you consider your own needs before theirs. I find a great naiveté in their [the reporters'] attitude that it's somehow sleazy to protect your own interests. I'm not denying that some businessmen take that to an extreme and say nothing when they could easily provide information, but I think it's far more complex than reporters are willing to consider."

In this day and age, an ill-chosen comment to a journalist can have potentially devastating results. A career could be terminated or restricted, a business badly damaged, or a personal reputation subjected to public criticism or ridicule. Even the most innocuous questions may be viewed as threatening to the interviewee. "You always have to be guarded," says Hughes, "always have to remember that anything you say, including jokes or other offhand remarks, could be quoted . . . maybe out of context. That's too bad, because it subtracts from the human relationship, the personal relationship between the journalist and whoever he or she is interviewing."

If you sense, or the guest tells you, that there are restrictions on what he or she can say, it is usually far more productive to negotiate what can be said rather than trying to bully the information out of the person. This decision hinges, of course, on whether you believe the guest is telling the truth. Even if the guest is lying, you win few battles in which your objective is to force someone to divulge information against his or her will. However, if you indicate a willingness to understand your guest's position, he or she may counter with an offer to tell you as much as possible, which may be more than you'd have obtained if the third degree was applied.

d. SOME OBSERVATIONS ABOUT INTERVIEWEES

From dealing with hundreds of interviewees in media seminars, I offer some random observations on the interview process from their perspective:

(a) It is not unusual for an interviewee to be unclear about the purpose of the interview until the story is published or broadcast. This is caused by two reasons: one, the interviewer or researcher is often vague about what the interview is actually about; and two, the guests don't ask. The latter comes primarily from their uncertainty that they have a right to ask. In fact, their passivity in allowing journalists to walk all over them is astonishing. They answer questions without knowing the context within which they are asked. This often results in damaging quotes appearing without adequate qualification. After the fact, if they feel abused and exploited — which many do — they lose their taste for talking with journalists.

(b) The interviewer is often perceived as an expert on the subject under discussion, despite all evidence to the contrary. As long as the interviewer is aggressive and has an air of assurance, many are willing to concede his or her superiority. In mock interviews, I find subjects will agree to made-up (and damning) facts and theories as long as I speak with conviction.

(c) I am appalled at how unwilling interviewees are to voice an opinion, even when it is blatantly obvious that they will look ridiculous if they refuse to comment. Many state emphatically that their jobs will be on the line if they stray even an inch from the prescribed company line. I have concluded that for interviews with people not designated to discuss policy — in government or business — it is crucial to negotiate ahead of time about what can be said to avoid wasting time by going to the wrong person.

(d) Few subjects see the interview as a two-way process. They identify it more as an interrogation, with the interviewer having to work for the responses. Rarely do they volunteer information. Unless a question is asked, crucial points are often withheld. This is done both out of malice and innocence, the latter the result of not being aware that they, as well as the interviewer, can introduce information and ideas.

(e) Few people are willing to say, "I don't know." There is a real dread, especially with government officials, of admitting ignorance. The result is a predisposition to use gobbledygook and long evasive answers which make them look worse.

(f) There is generally a lack of understanding of the broadcast media and a real fear of performing. Few understand the deadline and airtime restrictions, despite being avid consumers of TV and radio. Once the reason for the 30-second clip is explained, many try to accommodate the need for short, precise answers.

(g) There is a fairly universal feeling that the cards are stacked against interviewees when it comes to how they perform. While reporters can edit, do voice-overs, and fix their mistakes, the interviewees have no such luxury. "We don't get to rehearse, write a script, do it over. In fact, the worse we look, the happier they are," is an oft-heard remark. Many suggest that if they were given a second chance at an answer, they could say it better.

(h) Although they are more intimidated by television, interviewees fear print interviews the most, perceiving that the reporters totally control what and how information will be used. Radio is considered the least threatening.

(i) While there are those who resist being given an explanation of how the system really works, many are willing to accept and work with any information provided them. They appreciate any guidance that demystifies the interview, recognizing that it is to their advantage to understand as much as possible. I believe it is worth providing, when appropriate, as much information as you can about what is really taking place. If you collaborate with the guest rather than automatically setting up an antagonistic and separate relationship, there should be benefit on both sides.

e. INTERVIEWEES TALK BACK

Interviewees rarely get a chance to express their opinions about how the interview process feels from their vantage point. The following excerpts are from interviews conducted for this book.

Dirk Benedict is one of the stars of the extremely popular TV series *The A-Team*. A journeyman actor who has suddenly found himself hitched to a comet, he is now a highly sought-after interview subject. Articulate and confident, he describes himself as "basically intuitive," willing to dive headfirst into an interview and trust his ability to come out ahead:

> I prefer broadcast interviews because you can't be misquoted. And because I think I can communicate between the spoken words — gestures, inflections, sense of humor — a great deal that's hard to communicate in the printed word. It takes a very good writer to capture the real spirit of an interview. Usually all they capture is the intellectual aspect of it, the verbal part. They don't portray the emotion, at least very seldom. They certainly don't go near the spiritual thing or the sentimental or psychological environment in which it took place. I've read interviews sometimes that I've had and they're very dry. You wouldn't realize there had been laughter.
>
> By and large, I enjoy television interviews immensely, because I am in control. There's nothing they can do to keep me from saying whatever I want to say. I always say, "Ask me *anything*. It's not going to matter." I can make a joke out of it, avoid it nicely or I can ask the interviewer a question [about it].
>
> When you get to the printed word, quite often you get people who are wonderful writers but they are terrible at talking and asking questions. I've often felt that print interviews are much more revealing about the interviewer than the interviewee. One thing I wish they would do more is practice the art of conversation. Some of them are very good, but by and large there's an inability to create the atmosphere where someone being interviewed is comfortable.
>
> I don't mind answering "the same old questions" because it never comes out the same. There's always a different slant, because it all depends on who's asking the question. Nobody asks the same question *exactly*

the same, unless it's something really banal, like, "How did you get on *The A-Team?*" I feel you can even take that and turn it into something else, spring off into another direction. So I look at the same question as always being a different question, if you know what I mean.

Ed Arundell is the former manager of public affairs at Abitibi-Price, Incorporated, the largest pulp and paper manufacturer in Canada. A Ph.D. in political science, he's a former legislative assistant to Conservative Member of Parliament John Fraser. "I was a student radical . . . I've thrown my share of bricks at embassies," he says, indicating that his views on the media are rooted in a liberal background:

> Look at the average salary of a young journalist, maybe in the $15,000 to $20,000 a year range to start. He or she is assigned to interview a mill manager who may be making anywhere from $65,000 to $105,000, depending on the significance of the facility. They're sitting there in an environment that seems overpowering and there's an asymmetry already. Now, if it's one that both parties understand — that there are shades of meaning and bias that may come into play because of this — and they are attuned to that, then the interview can go more successfully. But if they're not, there's the potential for many things to go wrong.
>
> I'm a little troubled when I run into journalists who think they have to create the entertainment value of an interview on the basis of confrontation . . . to set up a dichotomy. On the basis of we-they, us-them, the public versus the industry. That's a real problem because what I see from my desk so very often is that a journalist will come in with a preset notion and really miss the story. May even miss a story that is sitting there waiting for him, one that has more news impact. Not necessarily one that will be a plus for us, either. Because of that "I've-got-to-get-him" mentality, they'll miss it, or miss the kernel of the real story

behind the situation. The "getting them" view sometimes blinds them to things that are lying right in front of them.

We train our people to understand how the media works. It's not a question of avoidance, but a question of preparation. Know what you want to say; what the message is you want to get across; what makes it worthwhile for you to do the interview; how, either in a very benign interview or a very combative one, you get your point across.

Look at the people who employ the journalist. It would be very rare for them to send in a cub reporter, a first-year graduate of journalism, to do the major feature of the year. They'll send in one of their top people, because he's been trained, has the skills, knows how to probe, knows the point of view he wants to get across. By the same token, I think the company has the right, the political party has the right, the government has the right to prepare its people to be comfortable in an interview and really focus on the points they feel are essential.

I think it's important to realize that more and more companies are going away from hiring former newshounds as PR guys, the types who try to manipulate the media. They are now going toward the person who is skilled in what the media is all about, whose emphasis is not to protect the company from the media but to prepare it to deal with communications in the twentieth and twenty-first centuries.

As a parallel to the whole move toward excellence, there's a greater emphasis in large industries on becoming more open in their communications. This forces managers to become interviewers, to learn how to probe, to learn how to have good communications skills in a small group meeting. That kind of training is just burgeoning in the industrial sector. The kinds of skills you need in the new era are listening, presentation, and humanizing training. They are not dissimilar to the skills you need for media training. So journalists are going to start encountering a more sophisticated type of businessman, one who may be more prepared for the interview than they are.

Lynn Johnston is the creator of the widely-syndicated cartoon strip *For Better Or Worse*. Each year she embarks upon a book tour to promote her latest collection of strips. Because the nature of her work changes little from year to year, inevitably the same questions pop up on each book tour. Friendly and open, she says she tries to be "a good interviewee," but doesn't always find it easy:

> I am constantly asked the same questions — when did I start, where do I get my ideas from, how far in advance do I work, are the characters based on my family — and it's getting rather monotonous. A great deal, though, depends on the interviewer. Some [interviewers] can make those [questions] interesting, can help me by their energy or enthusiasm. But many ask them as if it's the first time I heard them. I would rather we sat down and tried to come up with a way of doing the interview that satisfied their needs and made it a little more interesting for me.
>
> Some of them are primarily interested in showing you that they're a neat guy, really with it, especially on radio, where they like to be the person who has the crazy character. And they like to be very opinionated. Sometimes they put you off so much that, although you want to be a good interview, you can't.
>
> Most of the agony is television. A lot of times they want me to draw on the show and sometimes you can and sometimes you can't. Rather than saying, "Well, would you like to?" — I might be up that day and say sure, or I might be down and say no — they'll say, "Well, here's a drawing pad," without asking me in advance. And then they say, "And how's the kids anyhow?" They want me to draw and they want me to talk at the same time, which are two separate things and it's almost impossible. They think because I'm a cartoonist I should be able to draw and keep a

constant flow of dialogue at the same time, because they've only got so much time and they want to fill it.

Now and then it surprises you that you'll get a very friendly, warm interviewer and the article will be very caustic and unkind. On the other hand, you'll get someone who is sullen and cold and you think, geez, here's someone who eats lemons right off the plate, and it turns out to be very positive for you. You can't really tell, which makes it hard to feel comfortable.

One woman reporter from the *Calgary Herald* wanted to know how much I made. We were having lunch together. I said, "Look, I don't mind telling you, and it's from me to you, but it's really nobody else's business." And I said, "Besides, I don't want my kids kidnapped." I told her I was making about $100,000 a year at the time, which really isn't that much. Well, I wished she had put that figure in because what she did put in was much worse. She wrote, "Johnston will not divulge her income because she doesn't want her children kidnapped." It was the most irresponsible thing that anybody could ever have said because it looked like I was making millions.

Richard Gwyn, syndicated political columnist and author, on the toughest question he's ever been asked:

It was during the book tour for *Northern Magus* (an analytical biography of Prime Minister Pierre Elliott Trudeau). I was being interviewed by this girl TV interviewer in Edmonton and I'm all set to launch into my pat spiel of anecdotes when, as a first question, she asks: "Now, Mr. Gwyn, you've just written this book about Pierre Trudeau. Is it true he's a homosexual?" I got quite mad and sputtered out some answer — I don't remember what it was, but it was sufficient to deny the point and show my outrage that she'd asked it — and I was really quite close to walking off the set.

Judy Rebic of the Ontario Coalition for Abortion Clinics is an outgoing and energetic woman, with a strong, booming voice. Because of the volatility and profile of the abortion issue, she is interviewed frequently and seems to enjoy matching wits with an adversary:

I think I've built up a relationship with almost every reporter who's been on this issue for a long time. The importance of developing a professional relationship with the reporters is key, because they develop a trust relationship with you. They know that you don't bullshit them and that you are as accessible as can be. That develops over a period of time. And I think that's important for the reporter to know [that we want a relationship].

The biggest problem is when a reporter has a set idea in his or her mind and is only looking for proof or specific quotes for whatever their theory is. I'll give you examples of opposite approaches. The religion writer for the *Globe and Mail* called me. I'd never talked to him before. He said, "I've got a copy of the *Catholic Register* and I want to read you what it says." And this was the call from Cardinal Carter for Catholics to mobilize in front of the Morgentaler clinic. "What's your comment?" he asked. He didn't have a set idea in his mind about what he wanted me to say. If he'd asked me a specific question, he may not have gotten as good a story. What he did was say, "Well okay, this is really going to shock her. I'm going to read her the story and see what her reaction is." Another reporter had an idea in his mind that there was a division in the abortion movement, which there wasn't. And he really probed to find this division. And what he came out of the interview with was that we were worried about losing support and that our movement was being demobilized, which isn't what I said.

I get misquoted all the time but it usually doesn't matter. I've seen things I didn't say, written in quotes. It's not the words I used, but as long as it's the meaning, the context, it doesn't bother me. But one thing you always have to remember is that you're talking to a reporter, no matter how chatty they are and how friendly they are. And that takes training as an interviewee . . . that you're not going to say anything you don't want to see in print.

Some reporters come on with, "I'm your friend," which I don't like either — trying to indicate that they're on your side, so you'll tell them something. And I don't know if a reporter who is strongly on our side is any better for us anyway. I've found that some reporters, if they're strongly pro-choice, will overcompensate for it. They know they are prejudiced in a certain direction. And in trying to be "objective," they slant it the other way.

I think it's very important for interviewers to realize that they have a point of view and the person they're interviewing has a point of view. And if they are to be good reporters, they have to see the other person's point of view. They don't have to agree with it. But if you can't see the other person's point of view, then you can't be a good interviewer. All you're doing is fitting the other person's quotes into your own framework.

Dr. Alex Morrison spent 25 years with the Health Protection Branch of the Ministry of Health and Welfare in Canada, a good portion as the Assistant Deputy Minister. During his time in Ottawa, Morrison was constantly on the hot seat over some of the major health issues of the day. When dealing with bureaucrats, he says, reporters have to learn the intricacies of the system.

My dealings with the media evolved greatly over time. I wasn't trained and I'm still not trained to deal with the media. I was trained as a biologist and a scientist and all of a sudden, there I was, forced to deal with the media and not knowing how to do it. I've made every mistake many, many times and have just learned a little by trial and error. I didn't know how to behave, and I have to admit that I was scared out of my mind half the time.

Reporters have to understand how the political system works. And they have to know its complexities and subtleties. If they don't, what they will get from civil servants will be the blandest of blah, especially at the highest levels of the civil service. The relationship between the minister and the public servant is really a love-hate relationship. There's a great mutual respect, but there's also a kind of envy and jealousy that goes on. The minister envies the public servants their expertise. The public servants envy the minister's power.

You can get them at odds with each other very easily. Under those circumstances, the public servant, if he thinks he's being left naked or that his minister won't like what he's saying, will simply pull back into his shell and give nothing of significance.

I was often constrained by what I could say. I couldn't tell the whole truth, but I would not lie. I remember the day we canned the swine flu vaccination program. Marc Lalonde [then Minister of Health] made the announcement at a press conference. I went with him, stayed off camera to the left to whisper technical information to him. And as soon as he finished making his statement, all six cameras swung to me and they said, "Now Dr. Morrison, tell us the real truth." I was embarrassed beyond belief. It was total humiliation. Lalonde jumped up and waved his arms and said, "No pictures, no pictures." And I was in a position where it looked as though I was being publicly disloyal to my minister, and there's no greater sin than that for a public servant.

Now, if you take a more subtle approach, you can get a lot more information. [One reporter I knew] was very, very good. Without pushing, without drawing clear battlelines and without being combative, he got a great deal of information out of the system. He would ask questions in a way that didn't trap you, didn't make you feel you were going to be put in an impossible situation if you were quoted. He realized the importance of building up trust, over time, so you would be protected if you confirmed certain information to him. There's a way of speaking that will get you much further ahead than coming on too strong or trying to threaten the person.

The biggest lack reporters have is in technical understanding and in accepting the grayness of issues. They wanted to know: is a product safe or isn't it? These are the kinds of questions that are difficult to answer with yes or no. They had a constant problem of looking at very complex issues very childishly. And that's hard for a scientist who's been trained all his life to think, not in absolute terms, but in probabilities and uncertainties and tentative positions which are always changing as the evidence changes. It's very hard for [scientists] to come out and say yes, yes, no, no. We often felt frustrated by that.

I always felt it was useful for the journalist to talk to me in a background sort of way first. Before the interview started, we might talk for about half an hour because I recognize they can't be specialists. This would give both of us some perspective about where we were coming from. Those tended to be much better interviews.

Sam Hughes is the former President of the Canadian Chamber of Commerce. He speaks positively about his relationship with journalists, but is not without his criticisms:

One of the biggest problems for us is that of compression. Reporters want statements in black and white and, for television and radio, in 25 seconds. It's not possible to compress reaction to a complex subject in the time frame the journalist wants. I prefer when the journalist tells me he's only going to use a tiny clip. That way I can at least try my best to provide one. I think it's only reasonable to be told that.

Every time I move to a new city, I take the local newspapers and sit down one evening and take a red pencil and circle the adjectives on the front page. And some of those papers are extraordinarily covered in red pencil circles. Others simply present the facts. It's a fun exercise. You don't do anything with it. But when a reporter comes from the newspaper which uses adjectives, you have a bias in your mind. When a reporter comes from the newspaper that doesn't, you're much more open in your perspective.

Jack Webster has one of the most famous voices in Canada. Known for his outspokenness, his broad Scottish accent has been heard for three decades in Vancouver, on radio talk shows and now on television, exhorting politicians and other public figures to answer his passionate and direct questions truthfully and openly.

I interviewed him a few months after his wife had died, and rather than the rambunctious Webster of the public image, he was subdued and thoughtful. The interview reminded me to look beyond the stereotype, for I had called expecting to have Webster "perform" what I presumed were his usual rants and raves:

I was brought up in one of the blackest industrial cities in the world [Glasgow], where social injustice was a way of life. It was a great place to be a newspaperman in the thirties, I'll tell you. We had three evening newspapers, five morning newspapers, two Sunday newspapers.

We had a killing every Saturday night, and they always left it to us at the *Sunday Mail* — the police were really quite brutal — to break the news to the family. First of all, you'd wake the neighbors so that you'd have four or five women to support you. The moment they saw a reporter they knew there was excitement, disaster or tragedy. Then you'd knock on Mrs. Valaitis' door — I always remember her name — and say, "Mrs. Valaitis, I'm Jack Webster from the *Sunday Mail*." "Ohh . . ." "Your husband's been injured in a gang fight." "Ohh . . ." "As a matter of fact, he's dead." And then you'd buy the wedding picture off the wall. Ah, that was brutal . . . the picture snatching . . . I could never do anything like that again. I object to television showing people dying, I object to bodies being hoisted about on television. I believe in private grief.

(This led to discussion about what was the most important characteristic for a reporter to have.)

I think the mechanical skills are important. But overall, I think you need a broad education containing a sense of social injustice — that is imperative for a reporter. Everybody is full of biases. You and I know you can slant a story any bloody way you want to. Things are misquoted, inaccurate, cut, edited. I'm not saying you can overcome those kinds of things because of the nature of the business . . . but you should be as aware of your biases as possible, and care for the bloody people you're reporting about!

FEATURE INTERVIEW: Maureen McTeer

Many journalists in Canada saw former Prime Minister Joe Clark and his wife, Maureen McTeer, in a negative light. He was the awkward and conciliatory "Joe Who," the antithesis in style and demeanor to the elegant and confrontational Pierre Trudeau. She was the abrasive and defensive "women's libber," determined to use her own surname, and so unlike the indiscreet media groupie Margaret Trudeau.

McTeer was known in the media as a "bad interview," a cold and aggressive subject who not only refused to play the game by the expected set of rules, but was more than willing to launch an attack of her own at any journalist who provoked her ire.

She rarely talks to the media anymore, but readily agreed to a telephone interview that offered her the opportunity to discuss her views on the profession. Her voice was edgy and she seemed humorless, but there was also a naive vulnerability to her that suggested a softness struggling to come through.

PM: What is your general view of the media?

MM: I think the tendency is toward a very personal style, very people-oriented, very little attention to substance. If you look, for instance, at profiles that have been done on various people, if there was one thing that was an issue, there was no variation from that issue. It was as if everyone had read what the first person had written and whether it was true, false or whatever, they repeated it. Gave it a life of its own.

PM: Is that what happened to you?

MM: I think a lot of that happened to me. For instance, right off the top, I remember on the night of the 1976 leadership convention, a woman reporter came up to me and said, "Who are you?" And I said, "Maureen McTeer," and she said, "Oh, and what did you do on this campaign?" "I am the new leader's wife." And she said, "Oh, I didn't know he was married. Where is he from?" I said, "You have just covered this convention for the last two months. How could you not know anything about the person who just won?" She said, "Well, we didn't think he was going to win, we thought Brian [Mulroney] or Claude [Wagner] would." I was astounded. That was the first time I came into contact with people who could actually have a profession where they didn't have to do their homework.

PM: You mentioned the "one issue," and with you I guess it was your surname.

MM: What amazed me was that we had always been portrayed as Neanderthals because we were members of the Conservative party, and now an issue was being made out of something that to me was very normal, modern. The interpretation was, in the most pejorative way, that this was a "women's libber," and we all know that women's libbers are not nice people. Therefore, Maureen McTeer is not a nice person. So let us look for — and I'm always good at giving them reasons why they can say that — why she is not a nice person.

Why, she actually says to the press, "Buzz off," when they ask things like: are you pregnant? What does your husband like to eat? Or other dingbat questions like that. Or interviews became, "What's your stand on . . ." whatever happened to be the women's lib issue of the day. The most astounding question I was ever asked was when I was talking about food, about how I relaxed by cooking, and this reporter said, "You mean you actually cook?" I remember looking at the man and saying, "Even feminists have to eat."

PM: Did you become defensive in interviews, then?

MM: My response was just to stop doing most of them, becoming very choosy about who I talked to. I didn't expect everyone always to portray me in the best light. If I've made a mistake or whatever, I expect that to be commented upon. But I don't expect to be viciously attacked, for nothing. If it was just going to be the kind of situation where once again someone had the opportunity to define the person that I didn't think existed because it was easier than actually finding out what the person is really like, then I wasn't very interested anymore.

Because I don't consider myself to be an abrasive bitch, which is always what comes across. Because I have strong opinions, I'm intelligent, educated, then the assumption is that I'm domineering, that I'm everything pejorative attributed to women who seek to achieve. The human qualities, the caring qualities, the sensitivities are not even there because the assumption is that they don't exist, because the stereotypes don't have those qualities.

And fascinating, as you know, is that the assumptions then transfer to my personal life. Because in every personal life there "has" to be a dominant and a subservient. Therefore, my husband must have only subservient qualities. Which is fascinating because the very things which make him a great leader — his patience, his search for a consensus, his human sensitivity — are perceived as feminine qualities and add to this myth of subservience because they are not to be seen in a man, who has been defined in this kind of macho image.

108

I think what they [journalists] try to do is transfer their own prejudices or opinions of what a person in my position should be like or doing. I've done enough interviews that I can almost sense when I go into a room, after the first question, what the written interview is going to look like because of how the person is reacting to me.

PM: Do you think they were trying to attack your husband politically through you?

MM: Oh yes, and not just the media. People in our own party. But my husband's a very strong person, and I give him all the credit in the world. For when I was approached by people in our party to change my name — that the victory of '79 would rest on whether I was able to quickly enough transfer myself into a soft little kitten who called herself Mrs. Charles Joseph Clark — he told them to go to hell.

PM: Do you agree that when you are in a position such as yours, there's an interest in doing stories on you? Do you accept that they have a right to do profiles on you?

MM: Oh yes. I agree. But it's of no value if they're going to look at you exclusively in your role as spouse.

PM: Are you more comfortable with broadcast than print?

MM: I only do media now with people I have some trust with. I really have to know the people now or I won't even consider it. I usually try to do some research on the people who have requested an interview. Say if it's for television, I'll have a couple of their shows put on a VCR so I can get an idea of where they're coming from.

PM: Many people really enjoy the interview experience of having someone who's done his or her homework take an in-depth look at them. Have you ever felt pleasure at the end of an interview?

MM: Once. With Denise Bombardier in Quebec. She's the most prominent female Quebec television interviewer.

PM: And she put you through the kind of interview where you got something out of it?

MM: Very much so. I think it was partly because I had a greater respect for her intellect going in, because people whose opinion I don't respect had condemned her for being all the things they condemned me for. So I thought she couldn't be all that bad.

And also, because when I talked to her off the top — she has a son and I have a daughter the same age — we talked of more human things. Catherine, my daughter, has asthma, and we were discussing some of the problems I'd had the night before. I remember her talking about worrying about her son getting proper care while she was spending hours doing the program. We just seemed to click. And when we started the interview there was a kind of, not a friendship, but a mutual respect. And I think this was the key to it being an overwhelming success. Apparently they got calls and letters about what a good hour it had been.

PM: And did she ask you tough questions?

MM: Very tough.

PM: And that didn't bother you?

MM: I much prefer questions that are substantive . . . if they come from someone I have respect for. I just have a great difficulty hiding my annoyance when dealing with idiots.

PM: Do you read articles about yourself?

MM: Not usually. There was one done by a *Toronto Star* person last year that was incredibly bad. I think the headline was something like "I'm Wasting My Life," or something. I spent the whole time telling this woman all the things I considered to be of interest and value and was able to do now that Joe wasn't leader and how exciting it was for me to be in a position where every movement wasn't watched. And this huge headline was something like I was frittering my life away and I was just astounded.

PM: Was the article fairer than the headline?

MM: No. I had mentioned that one of the long-term projects I was thinking of was to take a business degree or master's in law at Harvard. I thought, Boston's quite close to Ottawa and we both love Cape Cod . . . and, for a term, Joe would commute as frequently as he could.

Well, immediately it was my marriage was falling apart, [reflecting] this preconceived notion that if spouses live apart for whatever reason or the female does something out of the ordinary, there is no relationship. It was such a self-imposed personal comment. I was just devastated that a woman who declared herself to be a feminist would be so myopic.

PM: When the media attacks on your husband were at their highest, did you sometimes think there was a conspiracy?

MM: I'm sure there almost was. I have no doubt about that.

PM: Your husband seems strong, but I wonder what effect the stories had on him?

MM: I'm sure they must have bothered him. I don't see how they wouldn't have. I don't know how he survived the last decade. I don't know how anyone could have survived going through what he's gone through.

PM: Do you think the root of the criticism was personal? Was his youth an issue?

MM: I think the youth certainly had a lot to do with it. A lot of the people writing were either the same age or older, who felt that they had probably reached the pinnacle of their careers and here was this young upstart from a small town in Alberta, heaven forbid, who had really made a life of learning the very system he hoped to lead.

I think the fact that he [did not fit] the media image of what a leader should look like had a bearing. That he should have the whole big shoulder and big jaw kind of mentality which seems to be so prominent these days. The glamor image.

And I think it was easier not to know what the region he was from was like. For instance, I would think that most people don't know that High River and all the ranches around it were owned by people from upper-class British families, who came over because they were the third or fourth son, because nobody knew what to do with them back home and they were a little bit wild and adventuresome. Some of them ended up in India, some in Canada. High River won the international polo championships in New York in 1939, and continued to have fancy dress balls and opera singers and all kinds of interesting, fascinating things happen. In fact, it's probably one of the most cultured places in the nation. . . .

PM: And they wanted to know if he could ride a horse?

MM: . . . and yet his inability to even be interested in riding a horse was seen as a reconfirmation of the fact that he was feminine. That he was not macho. I think the feminine thing was subconscious. What fascinated me was the refusal to say, isn't this a different type of cat? Let's explain what he's really like, where he's from. This was never done. It was always, he walks funny. He has no jaw. He's from High River, Alberta. His wife's too strong. All kinds of dingbat things that are so devastating because they don't challenge people to think.

5

PREPARING FOR THE INTERVIEW

Asking questions is risky business. Once you decide to look past the exterior, you enter potentially dangerous territory. The subject may not want to be presented any way but literally, and may not want content subjected to analysis. Anticipating your intentions, an interviewee may apply aggressive or seductive techniques to discourage you from your task. An interviewee may object to the intrusion and get angry at you, attacking from various directions. Not liking or agreeing with what you see, he or she may challenge your credentials, intentions, and personal or professional ethics.

The interviewer, says author Gay Talese, is a portrait painter, not a photographer. "I'm interpretive. I try to get inside the character I'm writing about very deeply. And I believe some of the truths of these individuals . . . are going to be revelations to themselves, when they read them, as much as they are to me when I discover them."

The goal in interviewing is not to dutifully snap the image presented, or accept information at face value. Rather, it's to search intelligently and compassionately for the essence of a person, or explore, with a critical eye, what he or she is saying. Instead of brushstrokes, the interviewer works with questions; and instead of colors, amplifies with tone.

There's another level of risk involved in asking questions. Because you come in contact with all types of people and their problems, you can't avoid taking on some of what they're going through. You might be able to con yourself into thinking that you're detached and just a passive observer, but if sparks are flying they'll be coming in your direction as well. "The sensitive issues were very painful for me," says Larry Zolf. "I used to get drunk every day when I was working on a documentary on loneliness. I couldn't take it. I preferred interviewing the powerful. Then I felt not guilty at all. I could be outraged and go after them. I was free."

"Judge a man not by his answers," says Voltaire, "but by his questions." While I applaud the philosopher's emphasis on the importance of questions, I believe both should get equal billing. Questions are not merely thrown out mechanically, like fishing lines, as bait for answers. They are far more powerful and significant. It may not seem this way for routine, brief, or apparently "meaningless" stories. But even in these circumstances, because you have to interact with someone else, your questions and attitude have the same potential to inspire, disturb, or otherwise affect a person as they would in any other situation.

What has to be remembered — and is too easily forgotten by interviewers — is that asking questions, in the context of journalism, is not simulated reality. On the contrary, it's all too real. But from my own experience, I know that in my enthusiasm or need to get a story done I can forget that. Somehow, because I'm working on a "story," it's not quite real life. Therefore, I don't stop to consider how my questions, angle, or end product affects the people I'm in contact with, or myself. It's full steam ahead, just get the work done. It's a hard discipline to remember that every question, like every shot on a golf course, is brand new, and has the same potential to land in the rough as it has to go straight down the middle, no matter how many times you've made the shot before. If you keep that in mind, not only will it improve the quality of your interviewing, it will also stimulate your interest. Each interview is an opportunity — "a gift," as Barbara Frum puts it — to discover information, other people, or yourself. That's why I love interviewing, and consider it a privilege to have such varied experiences.

a. PRINT VS. BROADCAST

With some trepidation, I'd like to make two sweeping generalizations: broadcasters are better interviewers than print reporters, and print reporters are more thorough journalists. There are many exceptions on both sides, but overall I believe these assumptions to be true.

Broadcasters, for obvious reasons, quickly learn to become skilled at the *techniques* of interviewing. Because their questions, tone, attitude, and body language could all be made public (some may be erased through editing, but you work from the premise that anything said might have to be used), and because of the requirement for structure and dynamics, great emphasis is placed on developing style. It doesn't take too many on-air humiliations to convince you that it's worthwhile to study the form.

Because no such demands are placed on print interviewers, many newspaper and magazine writers rely on their research and writing skills to pull them through. A story that hinges on a seemingly dull, unquotable guest can be enlivened by diligent fact-gathering and lively prose. But along the way, important information and sparkling quotes may be lost for want of the right questions being asked in the proper manner. (On the other hand, there is greater demand for accuracy and in-depth research in print. It's possible to bluff your way through a broadcast interview and rely on the guest to carry it, but no such luxury exists for a newspaper or magazine writer when he or she sits down and begins to compose.)

Many print reporters have never been taught how to interview, nor do they get any feedback once they begin. Thrown into a sink-or-swim situation, they usually don't drown, but they may not learn the most effortless or artistic ways of cutting through the waves. Bad habits can develop and may never be corrected. "Most print journalists can't stand the way they interview," says Roy MacGregor. "If you ever filmed a print journalist interviewing, that person would probably be laughed right out of his work."

This is not to idealize broadcasters; many painfully expose their poor listening and interviewing skills for all to hear and see. And the electronic media could learn much about content and how to dig up original stories from print reporters. Rather, my purpose is to call for a synthesis of the strengths of both groups. An interview, no matter for what medium, should combine form and content. When they are in harmony, the end result will be greater than when one of the elements is weak or lacking.

There are many different types of interviews, each with its own logistical demands and idiosyncracies. Questioning a witness to a robbery, for a brief newspaper article or TV report, is hardly the same as conducting a two-hour intensive probe for a magazine profile. Therefore, how you prepare relates directly to the nature and content of each interview. In this chapter we'll explore the points and procedures that are common to most situations.

b. THE STORY ANGLE

After gathering and sifting through whatever research is available, determine what angle — also known as a focus or hook — you want to pursue. If the story revolves around a 300-page tome on poverty and you have 5 minutes of air time or 750 words of copy, you can't talk or write about the entire report. Your story will need a point of view, a purpose, even if it's as simple as just highlighting the major findings. But it's usually more specific. Your angle might be to concentrate on poverty among native groups, or to compare poverty on a regional basis. If you cover a government budget, one angle could be an overview of the entire document, another might focus on social programs, another on the deficit, and so on. Whatever you select — and there are always numerous possibilities — the more directed you are before you go in, the better the odds that the interview will succeed.

For print interviews, it's not uncommon to go fishing, to embark on a long, rambling discussion in hopes that an angle will materialize at some point. However, it's a gamble you shouldn't take unless there's no other choice. Apart from the possibility that no angle will magically appear, the process can be a waste of precious time.

"To go in without a purpose is a terrible mistake," says Richard Gwyn, who has worked as a senior government bureaucrat as well as a journalist. "The more you put in the more you get out. Anyone who forgets that is a fool. If you don't know something you should know, something happens to the guy across the desk. You can feel it. From then on the interview goes downhill. The guy simply withdraws and thinks, why should I put out for this reporter? And then they treat you simply as a convenience, an instrument to get their message across. Or they avoid saying anything that will hurt them. You're always losing an interview for a reason. And that reason usually is that you've been lazy or you've relied on your native wit and it hasn't been enough."

For a broadcast interview, a predetermined angle is imperative. Because an audience sees or hears an interview only once (unlike a newspaper or magazine article, which can be read at one's own pace and referred to again), there is little room for confusion. Anything unclear disrupts the listening or viewing pattern and you may lose your audience, at least temporarily.

Information must be presented in an order that the mind can follow and absorb in one presentation. There is little tolerance for fishing trips that don't produce a catch.

The angle gives the interview a purpose, a reason for taking place. It usually occurs as a question. For a story on wife-beating, for example, many angles come to mind: Why do men abuse their wives? Is the behavior learned during childhood? Why do women stay with abusive husbands? How are the children affected? Is it an illness, a crime, or both? Can it be treated? What programs exist for wives, husbands, the family as a whole? Are the police and courts taking a tough enough stand? Do the police and courts tacitly condone wife beating through their reaction and sentencing procedures? How does society really view abuse of women?

Depending on the time or space available, a story on wife-beating could focus entirely on one of these points or encompass many of them. There can be several angles and sub-themes to an interview. For broadcast, how these connect is crucial. Structurally, the interview must progress in a style not unlike a play. There should be a beginning, a middle, and an end. For a live interview this structure must develop as it goes along. If the interview is taped, it can be rearranged after the fact, time permitting, but that's not always easy or possible. For print, the interview itself does not have to be structured, for the bulk of the work is in the writing. However, the need for angles and an interview strategy is just as important as in broadcast.

Journalism is basically the telling of stories. As any interviewer knows, nothing makes the bells of pleasure ring louder in the brain than a well-told anecdote or a clever analogy. Facts can usually be acquired on their own. But color comes primarily from first-person accounts. To draw out the best in a story-teller, particularly one who is inexperienced, you must provide an atmosphere conducive to the task. Your questions should inspire and assist in the telling, not interfere. If you guide a person's thinking or memory in a helter-skelter pattern, it makes it harder for him or her to remember or articulate. If you aren't an attentive listener, the quality of the person's "performance" will go down. Just remember how you've felt at parties when, in the middle of recounting an anecdote, you've lost the eye contact or attention of your audience. It's a sinking feeling.

The memory tends to work best when it's led in a chronological order. When interviewing former Canadian Conservative party leader Robert Stanfield for a documentary on the tenth anniversary of the War Measures Act, I started my questioning at the time before the act was invoked. I asked if he had considered terrorism in Québec to be a serious problem prior to the kidnappings by the FLQ (Front de Liberation du Québec), if there were incidents he remembered that shaped his thinking, where he was when he heard of the first kidnapping, and what his reaction was.

Although my main interest was his response to the invocation of the act itself, I wanted to warm up his memory by taking him back in time, away from 1970 and into the two previous decades. As I steered him toward my objective, I was careful not to shatter the reflective mood that had developed between us. By the time the critical questions came up, his memory was in full bloom.

There will be occasions when you deliberately want to be indirect and seemingly unstructured. A print interview allows the luxury of being able to approach an issue from many directions and at different times. A tricky point raised early in the conversation can be returned to at a later time. The same question can be worded slightly differently the second time, to compare how the answers jibe. This methodology is both planned and intuitive.

For "issue" stories, the angle is usually selected first, with appropriate guests contacted afterwards. With "personality" interviews, the order is invariably reversed. Finding a new angle is a difficult task at the best of times, but doubly hard when a frequently interviewed guest is the subject. This problem was faced by Robert MacNeil when he was asked by PBS to do a half-hour interview with author John Le Carré to accompany the TV series based on his book *Tinker, Tailor, Soldier, Spy*:

> I read everything he'd written about himself and all the interviews about him I could get my hands on. And I kept finding the same stories, the same anecdotes. Because basically the media is lazy, they just keep picking the same things up here and there. Now a certain amount of that I wanted, because it was good. Part of the exercise is to prompt a person to say, in a fresh and interesting way, for the television viewers who hadn't read all these magazine interviews or whatever, the interesting things he had to say about his mother and father, for instance. His father was a confidence trickster, constantly in trouble with the law and leaving them in houses with no money and then he'd disappear, go to jail, then appear again. I wanted him to say that, and he said it well. But I also wanted to try and get something this man hadn't been asked before.
>
> I finally came to it, the thing that wasn't there in other interviews, which was his attitude to women. Because all the women in the book, all the female characters — and this was before he'd written *Little Drummer Girl* — were women *manqué* in a way, they were deficient or somehow stunted. Particularly Smiley's wife. And so I wanted to know more about

that. What was it in his past, what was it in his attitude toward women, why were women never given heroic roles in the book? And he said, "You know, I've never really thought about that." And then he began to think, or at least he gave a very good impression of someone thinking originally about an answer. And I felt a little light go on and I said, "Hey, I like that." I don't remember all of the answer but it had something to do with his crazy upbringing.

Since *Little Drummer Girl* featured a strongish female lead, it's possible that MacNeil's question inspired Le Carré to take a new approach.

There is no formula for determining angles. Often it's nothing more mysterious than identifying the most obvious aspects of the story. But you should always be on the lookout for a new perspective, a way of avoiding the same old clichés. Put aside some time to think, without distractions, about how you might cover the story. This can be a matter of a few minutes or several days, with ideas rumbling around in your head, before the moment of insight is reached. Look for the underlying themes, not those that jump immediately to mind. Ask yourself what has been done about this story before and whether there is any value in repeating it. Then scan your intellect and imagination for questions that remain unanswered, hypotheses that have not been tested.

For the wife-beating story, for example, perhaps you could look at the widely held belief that the police and courts are powerless to intervene in domestic disputes. Are the hands of the police really tied? Or do they consciously or unconsciously believe that men have the "right" to beat their wives? This could be examined through interviews with police officers, legal experts, and women who have laid charges, successfully or in vain, against their husbands.

The essence of your approach should be to beware conventional wisdom. Eric Malling says he subscribes to the philosophy of two of his mentors:

Tony Westell [of the *Toronto Star*] and Ron Haggart [of *the fifth estate*] both share the same distrust for the conventional wisdom. Westell takes whatever people are thinking and turns it on its ear. When everyone was dumping on Trudeau for ruining the economy but saving the country, Tony came out with a book saying that, given the circumstances, Trudeau had done as well as anyone was doing with the economy but was ruining the country because of his approach to national unity. On almost any issue, whoever the pack is dumping on, Westell is defending and vice versa. As Haggart puts it, if it's one of those things that everyone knows, it's probably wrong.

Grabbing onto the easiest angle is a trait common throughout the profession, but seems to be of epidemic proportions in the coverage of sports. At the beginning of the 1985 NHL season, one of my students, having scalped the idea from a Toronto newspaper, wanted to do a story on the Maple Leafs beginning their new hockey season. The Leafs had finished twenty-first, a humiliating dead last, the previous year. Playing for Toronto is pressure enough at the best of times but it can be sheer hell when they're losing.

What the student wanted to write about was how eagerly the players awaited the new season. He had quotes to support his perspective from the newspaper clipping, and he was already well into the boosterism that so often passes for sports journalism. "How do you know they're all eager?" I asked. "Maybe half of them are dreading this year, praying they get traded. Maybe there's a psychological obstacle for them to overcome, getting psyched up for a new year in Toronto."

Investigating that angle, however, involves asking some unpleasant questions, establishing confidences with players, finding the right questions to draw out more than the usual pat answers. It's less complicated to have them produce nice quotes about another season being a new start, not to mention the fact that you don't want to be seen as

121

"disloyal" to the home team, a pressure that sports reporters have to cope with.

A final, but ultimately the most crucial, caveat about angles must be stated. The angle is not cast in stone. If during the interview something unexpected but important comes up, you may have to abandon your game plan and follow it. That decision will always be made on a case by case basis.

c. PREPARING THE QUESTIONS

There are various methods of preparing questions, such as writing them out verbatim or in point form, memorizing and/or rehearsing them, or just thinking about them. Or you could go in cold.

Broadcasters, for the reasons discussed earlier, are inclined to expend considerable effort working on the actual wording (although there are TV and radio interviewers who rely on their research and intuitive powers to carry them through). "A broadcast interview bears about as much relationship to a conversation as walking across the street has to do with a pas de deux," says Warner Troyer, elaborating on the need to prepare questions. "It is an enormously disciplined exercise." The demand for discipline is almost as great as it is for a theatrical performance. Just as a play is not a true representation of how people speak — it is far more precise, articulate, structured, and meaningful — so a broadcast interview must eliminate the excesses of speech and present a tightly woven interchange.

The conversation has to flow from point to point. Transitions must be logical. If an actress has just mentioned how the death of her young daughter almost made her give up her career, your next question cannot be, "Tell me about your favorite director." If you don't think it's appropriate to spend time on the death, you must at least acknowledge it, both for the sake of the guest and the audience. "You were able to overcome her death, however, and keep on working," you might say. "What made you decide to continue acting?" After her response, although you must be alert to the possibility that she wants and needs to speak about the death, it should be possible to move into questions about directors.

The same rule concerning transitions applies to print. If an interviewee raises a significant point, you can't just ignore it and head blindly toward the next question on your agenda.

Terence McKenna of *The Journal* and Pierre Pascau of Montreal radio station CKAC represent the two poles of thought about how assiduously you prepare questions. McKenna works methodically to hone his questions as tightly as possible, particularly for interviews he anticipates will be tough:

> I approach these confrontational or aggressive interviews a lot like a chess game, planning them out a great deal. The first thing I do is make a list of questions. Then I try to really put myself in their skin and think how they will answer. So I would block an interview out, saying, if I ask this question they will likely say that, in which case I can come to a follow-up question. Based on the answers, you are offered a choice of which way you can go. And then it becomes a game, a certain role playing. You really try to think of how they think, of what their answers will be.
>
> Then I will go back and redraft the questions and generally, if I have the time, I will rewrite and rewrite and rewrite the questions. Memorize them. And in that process, of course, what you can do if you don't want him to launch into his spiel is summarize [it] so that he can't do that in response to your question. That makes it easier to get him into the territory you want. In other words, in a real confrontation situation, it's a game of sort of pushing a man into a room where there are four doors. And you figure out which door he's most likely to go through and you try to close off the doors you don't want him to go through in the way you phrase your question. And then you push him into a room with three doors, then two and one, if you know what I mean. In the way you

approach, you try and keep him on your game plan so that he can't escape the points that you want to establish, that you want to have him answer. In an interview like that, I would spend hours thinking about what he could say, what I could say in response, and redraft my questions to do that.

Pierre Pascau takes the opposite point of view:

It's important to remember that we are interviewing, not interrogating. We are not the police. I don't believe that you have to have questions because then you're stuck with a plan. When I'm interviewing someone who is an expert in this or that field and they have a whole file of notes in front of them, especially in radio or television, I tell them, put these away because you cannot, at the same time, read your notes and talk to me in an intelligent manner. Put your notes away because if you don't know your topic you shouldn't be here. Let's have a conversation. Let's have a dynamic exchange.

If you have questions listed in front of you, you are stuck with those psychologically. You cannot move away from those, because you are not really listening to the answers, you're thinking of your next question. We interview people and we are not really 100% concentrating on the person we are interviewing, watching every bead of sweat on his face which could be telling you something and concentrating on the electricity between you. You must listen to what he is not saying, what he's trying to hide deep down.

My own preference is a blending of the two extremes, a mixture of rehearsal and spontaneity, with the emphasis on the latter. I begin by writing down the major areas I need to cover, producing a sort of blueprint. That guides me to the next step, which is jotting down some questions, in point form, in roughly the order I think they'll come up.

As this takes place, I often imagine how the interview might transpire. Years ago I plotted out moves and counter-moves with the cunning of a jealous lover. Now it's more casual — more to prepare than to defend. Rather than fixating on how to "win" the interview, my goal is to find the right questions, and the strategies to ask them. It's very similar to what I did in the past but with a definite change in attitude. The best self-protection, I've discovered, is to ask pertinent questions with the calm assurance that they deserve an answer. However, accomplishing that in an adversarial situation can require some intricate planning and foresight.

By mapping out the questions, key information and strategies emerge. How many questions do I have? What points are missing, weak, unprovable, or likely to be challenged? Where am I vulnerable to attack? Why? How do I respond? What questions require careful wording? What are the major transitions? What themes are emerging as the strongest? How prepared and confident am I?

This process, though, is not linear and clinical. It's not done to predetermine or ordain certain responses. It's much more fluid than that, a means whereby I become familiar with the subject matter, the guest, and my own feelings and ideas at the same time. Depending on the circumstances, I will go over questions and possible answers in detail, but more often than not, the greatest benefit of the imaginative process is to relax me. Rather than going toward the unknown, I feel more connected with what lies ahead.

As part of the exercise, using available information and my intuition, I try to imagine what the guest is thinking about the interview. Is he or she nervous, thrilled, opportunistic, terrified? What's in it for this person? How experienced is he or she with the media? By taking a few moments to consider the guest's perspective — and it's only a guess — I'm reminded that there's someone else involved in the interview.

I don't memorize the questions. When I've completed my preparations, I like to have time to clear my head so that when I do the interview I'm not restricted by some tyrannical plan. The information and rehearsal provides the confidence that allows me to trust that I'll know what to say and how to act in the moment.

d. THE OPENING QUESTION

Be it for broadcast or print, I place great importance on the opening questions. For myself, getting started is the hardest part. Once the interview begins to roll, I move with whatever is happening. So I focus much of my attention on how to generate that initial momentum.

If the right opening question is asked, it can turn a reluctant guest into an enthusiastic exponent, as Mutual Radio's Larry King discovered when he tangled with cantankerous physicist Edward Teller. Teller, who disdains most interviews, asked King, "How can you interview me if you don't know anything about physics?" King's reply — "I'm going to learn physics from you" — didn't convince Teller that he would enjoy the experience, but, with reluctance, he agreed to talk. "I led off the interview with the question of why, when I was in high school, I recoiled at the word 'physics'," says King. "His face lit up. He said, 'Because they shouldn't call it physics. They should call it life. Then he began to explain how it affected everyday life. We were off and running."

A tough, pointed opening question can also catch someone off guard. For a live hot-seat session with former Liberal cabinet minister Mitchell Sharp, Warner Troyer spent four hours debating the exact wording of the opening question with members of the *This Hour Has Seven Days* team:

> Sharp was gunning for [then-Prime Minister] Mike Pearson's job, lobbying behind the scenes for an anticipated leadership convention. We decided to give him a hard time. We argued extensively over what that first question should be. We agreed we should open with a tight close-up, what we call an ECU, where you would probably see his hairline and most of his chin but that was all. The screen would be filled with Mitch Sharp's face. And that picture would hang up there for all of the first question and the first response.
>
> As soon as the red light came on I smiled and said very softly, "Mr. Sharp, how long have you been working to take Mike Pearson's job away from him?"

And Sharp hesitated for about a double beat, he was so shocked. It was about two seconds. And what his face did and his eyes did in that two seconds were incredible. His eyes went "flick-flick-flick" from side to side and then up and down. You could hear the wheels turn and you could hear the synapses dropping in. Then he said that was a preposterous question, that he was completely loyal to his leader and all the appropriate things. And slowly, slowly the camera pulled back. But it was too late. In those two seconds he had done himself in.

The more sensitive or confrontational an interview, the more time I devote to the wording of critical questions. I don't want to endanger the interview or cause embarrassment by saying the wrong thing.

In 1978, I did a short documentary for *Morningside* on people who had lost 100 pounds or more at Weight Watchers. I had noticed a small ad in the newspaper announcing a banquet to celebrate the losers' victory and thought it would be intriguing to speak with people who had undergone such a significant physical and psychological transformation.

To prepare, I imagined what it would be like being fat, how, when, and why the weight accumulated, the struggles to overcome it, and how I would respond to my new self. Because most of the *nouveau svelte* were women, I spent much of my time imagining the unhappy lot of an obese female.

The next step was to develop questions that would be direct but not offensive or threatening. My decision was to begin each interview with the same question: "Were you overweight as a child or did you start to gain at a later stage in life?" That starting point was specific enough that the answer would give me vital information, yet allow people to begin their stories at their own pace, without being boxed in too tightly. And it passed the rather loose test I've established for my opening question: does it sound like a logical place to begin?

One of the main angles I wanted to explore concerned the relationship between self-image and weight and what role a spouse/lover had played. I sketched out some areas to pursue:

- What was your self-image when you were overweight?
- Why do you think you put on weight?
- Were you able to accept your size?
- Did you do anything to shield yourself from reality (avoid mirrors, photographs, certain kinds of clothing)?
- Did you avoid certain things because of your weight (parties, the beach, applying for certain jobs, speaking to attractive people)?
- Did you fantasize about being slim? How did you see yourself?
- What was your spouse's/lover's response to your weight? Did you believe he/she found you attractive?
- Did he/she make fun of you? Compare you to other men/women?
- Did he/she encourage you to reduce? When you actually followed through, was the support still there?
- Was he/she threatened by your new look?
- Did you become more assertive in the relationship? Did the roles in the relationship change?
- Did the weight loss and new attractiveness have any effect on your sexuality? (None of the women took offence at this because it was so directly linked to problems in their relationships. Neither of the men I interviewed was comfortable with it and I backed off right away. I had decided, during preparation, not to push this question unless the respondent encouraged me. I could tell by the tone, content, and body language of the answer how far I could go.)
- How has your life changed?
- Has it changed in the ways you expected?
- Do you ever feel, at some deep level, the need to become heavy again?
- What's your self-image now?

The interviews were a tremendous success. Caught up in the excitement of their "graduation," the interviewees spoke with candor and insight. "It was a lot easier than I thought," one woman said, "because the questions were the right ones to ask. I thought to myself, I wonder if he's been fat." (I haven't.)

e. IT'S NOT WHAT YOU SAY, IT'S HOW YOU SAY IT

Many years ago, I met an extraordinary person, a media artist who specialized in, among other things, listening skills. He became my mentor and we've since delved into many nooks and crannies of this perplexing profession, searching to understand what's really going on. One of our first lengthy conversations was about tone of voice in interviewing. I reproduce parts of it here, to the best of my memory:

Q: What can you tell me about tone of voice?

A: If you want to understand interviewing at anything more than a superficial level, you have to tune your ears to hear the virtual orchestra of tones every person has in their repertoire. All the information you need can be heard in the tone of voice. It may seem hard to accept, but if you listen at the deepest level, they'll tell you what to ask, where they're vulnerable, if they're lying, whatever is going on inside them. They might be able to manipulate their language, or at least think that's what they're doing, but they can't conceal their tones. The art, for the interviewer, is to develop what I call "superior insight," the ability to hear those tones and know what they are telling you.

Q: Can you give me an example of tones displaying meaning?

A: I saw an interview once with a so-called student radical. They blacked out his face to protect his identity. He was talking about demolishing the system, blowing people away, all kinds of tough talk. But his voice was full of fear and pseudo-aggression. I didn't think it took much insight to figure that out. Here was a "terrorist" who was more terrified than anyone else. But the interviewer didn't pick up on any of that, didn't address that, ask questions to draw that out. He [the interviewer] glorified the student, fed his ego with questions that anointed him instead of calling his bluff.

Q: What could he have said?

A: One thing would have been, "Despite all this tough-sounding talk, I hear a lot of fear in your voice. What are you afraid of?"

Q: Wouldn't it have been rather risky? What if the student completely denied it and challenged the interviewer to prove his point?

A: I don't think it would have been much of a risk. First of all, if you listened with any degree of insight, you could hear where he was. And second, he was asking to be challenged. Why else would he do the interview? Obviously there was a certain amount of ego gratification involved, but at a deeper level he wanted to talk about what was really the truth. He wasn't thinking that consciously, but it was pouring out of him in the way he was speaking, in his tones. It might have shocked him to have that mirrored back at him and he might have denied it hotly. But I guarantee you it would have been well worth watching how he did it.

Q: Perhaps in that situation the tone was easily decipherable. But isn't it usually more subtle than that? A lot harder to figure out?

A: No. In most cases it's relatively straightforward. It can be complex but that is the exception rather than the rule. The information, you see, is always there. People are always telling you what's happening with them. We all have gut feelings about what a person really means when he says something. So the process is not one of memorizing a formula whereby this kind of tone means aggression or that kind means ecstasy. The process is one of developing our listening to a point that we can actually hear the tones. When that happens, our intuition will guide us to what we have to say.

Q: How do you develop it?

A: The best way I know is to be as alert as possible to what's happening with yourself during the interview, your gut feelings especially. The more conscious you are of what's going on within yourself, the more you start hearing what's going on around you. Then you start experimenting, applying this new information during interviews. As you work with it, you will discover it adds textures, colors, dimensions to your experiences. It opens the door to where the real action takes place. Anyone can ask a list of prepared questions. You could have a robot do that. But to dive into the middle of the fire of human emotions and passions, that takes courage.

Q: Does that mean listening to your own tones?

A: It does, although I prefer to think of it as being aware rather than just listening. There's a tone to how you said that that suggests this is some technique you can use and manipulate to give you an advantage in this battlefield known as an interview. Listening to the tones helps you do the interview at a higher level. It helps you decide whether to be aggressive, assertive, when to back off, whether a guest needs help and support to tell his story. You can hear tensions, invitations, provocations, con jobs, self-aggrandizement, flirtations, a panoply of sounds that are virtually shrieking at you to be heard.

Q: Then why don't most of us hear them?

A: Because most people are asleep at the wheel! Also, because it's hard work. And it can be scary. Since the best way to hear what's going on with someone else is to listen first of all to yourself, that can mean seeing some things about yourself that aren't so pleasant. Not many people like to do that.

Another point I'd like to raise concerns fascination. If you approach an interview, never mind life, without a fascination for the world around you — particularly yourself — there will be a tired or uninterested or pseudo-aggressive tone in your voice that the guest will hear. It may be well camouflaged, but it will seep through at some silent level. Being aware of that fascination, however, takes discipline.

Q: What do you mean?

A: Unless you are disciplined and work hard at remembering the fascination of life, the memory can slip away. The daily grind will take over — the routineness of just another interview, another package of research. It can all start to sound the same. You can easily forget the uniqueness of each moment, each meeting of the minds. People who see the world in all its shapes and forms, who see people as more than just some product that may as well be on the supermarket shelf, are not lazy or undisciplined people. You know when you meet people like this, whose energy is radiant and powerful. They get that way, I've found, by bloody hard work. From struggle. Because it's easier to numb out. It's easier to see issues and people in black and white. It's harder the other way.

f. THERE ARE NO RULES, BUT HERE ARE SOME OF THEM

There is no handbook or manual that can tell you exactly how to ask questions. The spontaneous, unpredictable nature of the interview prevents that. However, there are some general principles worth noting:

(a) The longer and more convoluted the question, the easier for the guest to avoid answering it. If you raise more than one point in a question, the guest is able to choose which to respond to. If your language is muddled or complex, the respondent can throw it back in your face as a means of unsettling or ridiculing you. "President Nixon made a habit, in a tight spot, of diverting the reporter to repeat himself," says Dan Rather in *The Camera Never Blinks*. "By doing so, he accomplished two things. He had more time to think and he put more heat on his questioner. I saw President Johnson do that once and I marked the tactic then as one to guard against. A reporter posed a complicated question. LBJ gave him The Stare, then said flatly, 'Well, first of all, I don't think you can even repeat that question.' And the guy couldn't. He just froze. The room erupted with laughter."

(b) Ask questions rather than make statements. Although it occurs naturally in conversation, the question in the form of a statement is usually too vague and easy for the guest to reject, ignore, or avoid answering. It is prevalent in sports reporting:

Reporter: Great game, Bobby. (Translation: Tell me anything about the game — team, opposition, your highlights. Any quote will do.)

Jock: Blah blah blah. Team effort. Blah blah blah. Gave 100%.

Reporter: That was quite a catch.

Jock: Blah blah blah. Up in the air. More blah. Lucky to come down with it.

Most athletes know only too well their lines in this hackneyed script. Neither party has to worry nor do much work. The script has become so ritualized that it's no longer necessary to formulate questions. Simple verbal cues — "How about that missed field goal?" — have replaced probing questions. Not all sports reporting is mush, but there's enough to create a fairly soggy impression.

However, that kind of neutered questioning can easily backfire with those who haven't agreed to the script. If you ask an agitated businesswoman, "What about that new merger?," she's well within her rights to snap back, "What about it?" Apart from aggravating the relationship between you, the question is a waste of time. Even if she did answer, the content and direction of her reply would be entirely at her discretion.

(c) Don't answer the question for the guest:

Interviewer: I guess that new government legislation is really going to damage your company's sales in the U.S. Is that right?

Executive: Yes.

This nervous habit is extremely damaging. In broadcast it's lethal, but it's also destructive in print. You can survive a few of these by describing or paraphrasing what was said, but you also must have quotes from the source.

This type of question also irritates and alienates the guest. If you already know the answer, the guest thinks: why ask me? It signals that you aren't open to what the speaker has to say, especially if it diverges from what you seem to have predetermined.

(d) Don't say "okay" or "right" or some other affirmation after each answer. This is annoying to the speaker (and any audience) and suggests that you're not really listening. "A lot of bad interviewers come in with a series of questions and don't listen to your answers, they just tick them off verbally and go on to the next," says Pierre Berton. "That practice reminds you that this is an 'interview.' But it shouldn't sound like an interview. I always have some reaction to what the interviewer says, the way I would in normal conversation."

(e) Don't apologize for asking a question. If it's pertinent and fair, ask it directly (although this doesn't mean without sensitivity). For example, suppose a prominent politician has divorced his wife in a messy, public affair and is now living with his former secretary:

Interviewer: Maybe you don't want to answer this, I know it's rather personal, but I wonder if you could tell me why your marriage ended?

Politician: You're right. It is too personal. I'd rather not discuss it.

By providing the guest with a ready-made excuse, you are telegraphing not only that he or she doesn't have to answer, but also that you feel awkward about asking. Your wording implies that you find the question too personal and not really pertinent.

(f) Work on the wording of difficult or sensitive questions beforehand if you're not confident about how to phrase them. Some interviewers tell the guest in advance that tough questions will be forthcoming. Others preface the difficult questions with an explanation that certain points have to be covered. Many interviewers save awkward questions until the end," so as to beat a hasty retreat out the door with my quotes," as one of them put it. But that's not a hard-and-fast rule. I've found that asking the difficult question early on can often clear the air.

In the case of the divorced politician, if you decided his personal affairs merit discussion, you could use the following strategy:

Interviewer: There is considerable public interest in your private life. A great deal of attention recently has focused on the breakup of your marriage. Do you accept that, being a high-profile politician, your private affairs are going to become public knowledge?

This opening question demonstrates that you know it's uncomfortable for someone's personal life to be exposed in the media, but that for a politician it comes with the territory. It's also a means of getting the person to begin talking by allowing him to state his case. Once a conversation gets past the first hurdle, it tends to open up. By persistent but reasonable questioning, you can create an opportunity for the politician to explain his perspective on much broader issues: for example, how politicians cope with the public's projections of issues like divorce.

(g) Know how to rebut if the question is tossed back at you. If the response to your question is a question in return — "Well, what would you do?" — in most cases consider it a desperation tactic, a stalling method that should encourage you to continue in the direction in which you're heading.

The best response is to treat it as rhetorical and not say a word. Generally, if you stay out of it, the guest will start talking. If that doesn't work, avoid getting drawn into a reversal of roles unless there's no alternative:

Interviewer: Why hasn't your company taken any action to rectify this problem?

Spokeswoman: What do you think we should do?

Interviewer: That's really a question for you. It's your company.

Spokeswoman: But you have been sitting here pointing the finger at us. I'm asking you what these magical solutions are that you seem to think are so black and white?

Interviewer: I have to repeat that my role is to pose the questions. If you think the question is unreasonable or that you don't have an answer, you should say that. But to throw it back at me makes it look as if you're trying to avoid answering.

If this ping pong continues, there comes a point when it's unproductive and silly to persist. By that time the audience will have been able to reach its own conclusions as to who's fair and who's avoiding the issue. In a print interview, whether it's represented in your article depends on the context. In either case, there's nothing to gain and a lot to lose by getting trapped into becoming the respondent and not the questioner.

The best way to avoid being ambushed by a return question is to anticipate, in your preparation, where it might arise. Usually it comes in response to an accusation, judgment, or question that is so worded that the interviewee feels trapped. Someone who feels trapped and under pressure will try and fight a way out, using any weapon available.

(h) Don't be too quick to jump in with your next question. That often cuts a guest off who was just about to continue. Having the discipline to remain silent, even for a brief moment, will bring many rewards. If what you hear sounds unsatisfactory or too much like a packaged spiel, say nothing. Invariably, the guest will keep talking, because he or she figures that what was said wasn't sufficient and needs to be augmented. What comes out is often the real answer.

(i) Avoid sweetheart questions. Too many interviewers are sycophantic to a guest, especially a famous or powerful person. More often than not, the reason for doing so is nervousness or a feeling of inferiority in the presence of "greatness." By swaddling the guest in praise, the hope is that he or she will be friendly, cooperative, or say something nice to you. If you have genuine admiration and respect for someone, that can be mentioned, but let it come out in the quality of your questions and the energy and enthusiasm you put into the interview.

Don't gush or grovel. Most guests are uncomfortable in the presence of someone who is full of, "I'm just one of your greatest fans. I think you are so wonderful. Now tell me about yourself." That imbalance makes it difficult — for you and your hero — to perform with dignity. People speak best when there's some element of tension or challenge. Questions that ooze rather than stimulate or provoke will not accomplish that.

(j) Likewise, avoid the pseudo-aggressive questions at the other end of the spectrum. Such questions are also inspired by nervousness, masked in this case by trying to act tough. While it may bully some people into responding, in most cases it will elicit anger, silence, disrespect, or other negative reactions. It can create a hostile or unpleasant condition that wasn't warranted or necessary.

It's important to distinguish between rudeness and assertive persistence. "I think you have to be polite, but that doesn't mean you don't keep after someone who isn't answering your questions," says Roger Smith, formerly of Canadian Press and now with CTV. "A lot of journalists think that because they're in an antagonistic role with a politician, for example, they have to be tough and rude. I don't think you have to. I think you should conduct an interview as you would any other personal relationship."

(k) Don't say you understand an answer unless you do. One of the most common and self-destructive faults is to pretend you understand when you don't.

"A very powerful phrase is, 'I'm sorry, I just don't understand that'," *Globe and Mail* reporter Linda McQuaig told an interviewing seminar. Judy Nyman of the *Toronto Star* concurs:

> Sometimes you have to be able to ask the same question several times, especially if you're speaking to somebody who's talking technically and you don't understand it. If you say you do, you're going to be lost from then on in because they're going to build on that and the whole interview's going to be for naught. So you've got to make sure you've got the basics, even if it means you've got to say, "Look, I'm sorry, I know you've explained that to me three times already, but I honestly don't understand it. Let's go over it step-by-step." Now, if something is a very obvious question . . . that you think you know the answer to but you're not sure, I usually get around that by saying, "This is a basic question, but. . . .' Sometimes I use a little cop-out, like "I know the answer to this but I just want to hear it in your own words." I find it much more embarrassing to have to call somebody back after the interview and say, "I forgot to ask you this," or "I was just looking through my notes and I don't understand this."

This principle is particularly relevant when the subject matter is highly technical. If a scientist, for example, uses terminology or theories that you don't understand, you must admit your ignorance. Apart from ensuring that you produce an accurate story, you're properly representing the level of knowledge among your readers or audience. Chances are that, if you don't follow what he's saying, your readers or audience won't either.

With bureaucrats, the problem is usually one of translating their deliberately vague language, a special code they use to avoid giving specific information. You need to persistently ask for specifics.

(l) Don't be afraid to ask "simple questions." People often equate simple with stupid, which is a mistake. One of the hardest standards to achieve is simplicity. Anyone can avoid getting down to the essential points by camouflaging a story with all sorts of overblown language and complicated questions. Clarity and conciseness, on the other hand, is harder to achieve and requires considerable effort.

Many interviewers feel that asking "dumb" questions is the best technique. Wade Rowland, who is a producer with CBC-TV's *Marketplace*, has spent most of his 20-year career in journalism as a print journalist:

> To me the most useful technique in interviewing someone, especially someone in a position of authority, is to ask all the dumb questions, the most naive ones. You draw them out much better that way than if you try to impress them with how much you know about the subject. Whether you know it or not, you should ask the dumb questions because you might be surprised by the answers. You often will be. Often you'll find out that you don't understand it as well as you thought you did. And you don't have to look stupid. You can apologize for your questions and ask them anyway.
>
> Women, from my experience, do much better in interviews than men and it's for that reason. Their egos don't prevent them from asking dumb questions. People open up to them much more and try to tell them everything they know in very basic terms. You can play that role whether you're a man or woman. It

has nothing to do with feminism, macho or anything else. It's just a useful technique.

To me the most important thing that any journalist has to remember is to keep your ego under control at all times. Don't try to be a star. It warps the story. The story isn't you, it's somebody else and you have to realize that. It's a humbling realization that you are just a conduit for information. If you are any more than that you're not doing your job.

(m) Try to ask stimulating questions. While the simple questions are essential, so too are original and provocative ones. "Most questions are boring and lack any insight or creativity," says Roy MacGregor:

Boy, do I ever notice it in daily journalism. Whenever I read interviews with politicians, I sometimes wonder if I'm out of my tree because I would never ask *any* of those questions. I wouldn't waste my time or his time because you are going to get an answer that has been delivered in 35 speeches, that has been referred to 60 times over in the campaign. But too many journalists think the question and answer thing is an exchange for the record.

I see it as the only chance you are going to have to see if you can crack through the facade and let the true personality flow out, to try and get them to open up. I would go in and ask [Prime Minister] Mulroney, "So what does it feel like, when you wake up in the morning and there is that funny moment we all have when you might not realize where you are or what has happened. Or you are not even sure what age you are ... and then you remember that you are the Prime Minister? And what does it feel like to be the Prime Minister?" I wouldn't waste a minute asking a question there's already an answer for.

That type of question by freelance interviewer Lawrence Grobel incensed the rarely interviewed Marlon Brando in a 1979 *Playboy* profile:

Grobel: You once said that for most of your career, you were trying to figure out what you'd really like to do.

Brando: "You once said." There ought to be a handbook for interviewers and one of the don'ts should be: Don't say "You once said," because 98.4% of the time, what you were quoted as having said once isn't true.

(n) If an interview is eliciting nothing of value and you feel the reason is the attitude of the guest, you have nothing to lose by addressing that. If a guest is taciturn, hostile, or otherwise uncooperative, that state has to be dealt with or else the exercise becomes a waste of time.

The wording of the question depends on the particular situation, but some variations on the following might get the guest to open up:

"I have the impression that you're not happy with my questions. Is there a problem with what I'm asking?"

"I feel a great deal of defensiveness from you. I'm wondering if it's because you're nervous or because something is wrong."

"I need to stop at this point because I sense the interview is not going well. For my purposes I need to have you give more details, more information, but I don't get the feeling you want to do that. Rather than make this a meaningless exercise, maybe we should talk about the interview a little before we continue."

(o) Difficult as it may be, there are times when you'll need to interrupt. For broadcasters, interrupting is more critical. They don't have an abundance of time so a guest who rambles on indefinitely must be stopped. One method is to use body language (e.g., gestures of the hand and/or face) that you need to interrupt. Another is simply to butt in: "I'm sorry to interrupt but with limited time I feel we need to get on to another question."

For print interviews, it's usually easier to hang in there until you find an opening to jump in. However, someone who refuses to let you speak is employing a technique to control you. It's not simply some characteristic of their speech that has no purpose behind it. So if you comply and remain silent, the person is going to continue or escalate the tactic. You may have to fight, not just to get a word in edgewise, but to maintain your position of power.

(p) If your mind goes blank, which can happen no matter how experienced you are, there are several ways to recover. The first is not to become terrified by the few seconds of silence, even if it's for a broadcast interview. Take a moment and try and recapture your train of thought. The next is to explain to the guest that you've blanked momentarily and need a second to regroup. Quite often, the guest will help you out as in any "real" conversation.

(q) There is considerable controversy about the "How do you feel . . .? question." It's the one that seems to drive people the craziest, including author Pierre Berton:

> "How does it feel, Mrs. So-and-So, your husband has just been murdered and your children shot, how do you feel?" Well, Christ, you know how she feels. She feels bloody awful. You shouldn't be asking questions like that. There are better ways of saying it. You say, "Mrs. So-and-So, I know you've gone through a hard time and must feel like hell." You establish your understanding and you can do it with variations of that technique.

But Peter Desbarats wonders if the question is really so bad:

> I certainly wouldn't take the position that you should never ask it. I think that for television particularly what you've got to convey quite often is the emotion rather than the facts. Somebody has been through a tragedy, you're trying to really show how they feel. And it may be necessary to ask people how they're

142

feeling. I believe that the television camera and the interviewer at that point are playing a social role, which justifies a certain amount of intrusion into people's privacy, within limits. I mean, you've got to be careful. If you remain within those subjective limits a lot of people will accept that and will recognize that the journalists' curiosity is by proxy for society in general. And they can accept that a journalist can ask a prying question that would be horribly intrusive if it were being asked simply out of private curiosity. I'd be very uncomfortable saying that a journalist should never say, "How do you feel?"

(r) Bear in mind that many interviewees will only answer questions, not volunteer information. As a parting note, I always ask if there was anything I didn't ask that they think is important, or if they have anything they'd like to add. This can sometimes open the floodgates, as points they've wanted to make but couldn't bring up in response to your questions come pouring out.

FEATURE INTERVIEW #1: June Callwood

June Callwood has been a journalist for the past 45 years. She is a columnist, author (*Love, Hate, Fear and Anger* and *Portrait of Canada*), ghostwriter (including a biography of Otto Preminger and Barbara Walters' *How to Talk With Practically Anybody About Practically Anything*) and dedicated supporter of civil liberties and Canadian nationalism.

One of the most respected writers in the country, she has a reputation for fairness and commitment to social justice. Her hectic schedule only allowed time for a brief conversation one afternoon:

PM: Thanks for agreeing to do the interview.

JC: I don't have a lot of time. I'm off to the library to do some research for an interview I have tomorrow with Laura Sabia, for my column in the *Globe and Mail*. I've known her for 15 years but I wouldn't dare go in without knowing her whole biography cold.

PM: Are you a stickler for research?

JC: Very much so. My analogy is, if a mechanic is working on a car and a child comes up and asks what he's doing, the mechanic says he's fixing the car. That's enough of an answer for the child. And if a neighbor comes along who knows a little bit about cars, the mechanic might say he's fixing the camshaft. But another mechanic who comes along — someone who knows the subject — is going to get a very interesting answer about what's wrong with the car. I spend a lot of time in libraries doing research so that for interviews I can be the informed mechanic who comes along.

PM: Do you have a philosophy about interviewing?

JC: I always thought the only way to have a successful interview is to be trusted and liked by the person you are interviewing. I don't know any other way. Everybody, if they like you, will tell you more. You can turn people on just by listening to them, really listening. And through questions that draw them out more and more. It's intoxicating. Almost everybody will tell you more than they mean to . . . they forget you are a journalist.

PM: What do you do if they've told you something you think will hurt them, during this moment of intimacy?

JC: I don't run things if I think people can't live with them. If I know they've said something they couldn't live with, I wouldn't, no matter how wonderful or sensational it is. It's not worth it.

PM: What if they damn themselves?

JC: When people are foolish, that's different. I have interviewed people who are bigots and pompous and they say bigoted and pompous things. I just quote that straight out. That's the way they are and that's the kind of person they are. But what I'm talking about is someone who's telling you about his family life and stumbles on to telling you

144

about a teenage suicide and you know he just wanted to talk, not to have it in the newspaper. I might say, "Is this what you want me to say. Are you sure?" If he responds, "Oh my God, please don't," then I don't.

PM: Is there something about you that makes people want to talk to you?

JC: I think that I have always been trusted. I know that's true. And it's an enormous advantage. And now that I'm older and have a reputation for being trustworthy I'm very rarely turned down for an interview.

PM: Do you plot interviews in advance, role-playing them?

JC: No. I'm really prepared but I don't role-play or anything like that. I usually tell them what material I want from them or what areas I intend to cover. It may be something very specific. If it's just a long fishing trip to see what's going to happen, then I ask about the parameters of time. How much time do we have? Two hours? Fabulous.

PM: What interests you about interviewing?

JC: I'm most interested in the underlying. I want to understand how people put themselves together. The most interesting series of interviews I did was when I was doing columns for the *Globe and Mail* called "The Informals" in the late 1970s. I did them for maybe two-and-a-half years. They ran every two weeks. And I asked everybody the same questions. I made up a list of 20 or 30 questions, a grid, and what I was after was how people formed their ethic. It didn't work with people who were charlatans or chameleons or psychopathic — empty. But with a person who had a center, you could address that center, and it might be guarded as of course all our centers are. But if you can find a way of asking questions that reveal, that get at how the center was developed, you can understand people's behavior better.

PM: What were some of the questions?

JC: The first question was always, "Tell me about your grandparents," because most people have a very strong tie and are very open about their grandparents. It's not as threatening as talking about parents. Because our grandparents form character in us in a way that's different but almost as powerful as parents. People always lit up to that question. If I asked you about your grandparents, would you be interested in that?

PM: Well, I don't really have any memory of my grandparents. Both my grandfathers were dead before I was born and my grandmothers died when I was too young to remember them. I regret not knowing them. In fact, I've had little contact with my extended family most of my life. I have virtually no relatives in North America outside of my immediate family.

JC: You see the interesting areas it leads into. I would follow that up, your feelings about extended family, if I were doing the interview with you.

PM: What else did you ask?

JC: The key ones would be, "When you're lonely, what do you do about it?" I never say to someone, "Do you have problems with loneliness?" because everybody does, but they'll tell you no if you ask them that way. "What do you do about being lonely? How do you cope with it?" People rarely deny that they're lonely if you say it that way. Another question was, "What is it about people that impresses you most when you meet them?"

PM: By telling you about others, they tell about themselves?

JC: Right, of course, that's the point. I ask about sleeping. "Do you sleep well, and if you don't, what do you do at 4 a.m. when you're still awake? What do you think success is? As a young person, what were you afraid of? How did

146

school go for you, were you bullied?" The usual sort of pop psychology questions. And all in an hour. Each interview was the same length.

PM: Do you have to be willing to open up to have them open up?

JC: I don't believe in this "let's cosy up and have an exchange" approach. Priming the pump with someone who's having trouble with her teenage children by saying, "I've had the same trouble with my teenagers." Exposing yourself — no, that's dishonest. It's like the policeman not wearing the uniform. It's a professional relationship you're having. I don't like this, "Now we're buddies, tell me everything about you."

PM: Then what kind of relationship do you establish?

JC: I make it clear: I'm the interviewer, not your friend. I make it clear I'm not going to betray them that way. And I tell them, I will not deliberately distort who you are, as much as I can know who you are. And I'll certainly never misquote you. I always read people their quotes. Always. When I write the piece I phone them and tell them, "This is what I've got in quotes."

PM: Do they ever try and change them? Vet them to suit their purpose?

JC: Sometimes. They'll say, "I wish I hadn't put it that way." And if it's a reasonable change I usually go along with it. If it's something that could really hurt someone, I might say, "Well, let me tone it down," but I wouldn't take it out if it were necessary for the piece.

PM: What about quotes that really make someone look bad, in a critical story?

JC: I find if you read a bigot his quotes, for example, he usually says they sound fine, because that's the kind of person he is. Reading people their quotes rarely causes any problems.

PM: Do you ever become aggressive?

JC: There's no point in creating hostility in an interview. I never found that useful. I will challenge people. I will say, "I'm having trouble believing this. I don't know whose problem this is, yours or mine, but this story doesn't seem to hang right to me, it doesn't feel right."

PM: Do you have any problem asking tough or extremely sensitive questions?

JC: No. Assuming the person can handle it, I ask the hard ones in a straightforward manner. I think that's a respectful way of doing it. If the person has been shifting and sliding or charming or wary or whatever, I guess I would try and find a way to phrase the question that wouldn't raise the hackles too much. I would say, "This is what I know and I have to know from you whether my version of it is right." When you get to the awful ones, I don't think you can do that until they like you. No one will tell someone they don't like anything important about themselves. So they need time to size you up. That's a reason to wait until some time has passed in the interview.

PM: Is it an advantage being a woman interviewer?

JC: I think it's an enormous advantage being a woman interviewer of men. Because a male interviewer, excepting the androgynous ones, get into a competitive relationship with male interviewees. They don't relax with one another. They try to see who's top dog. That doesn't happen with a woman interviewer and a man.

PM: Barbara Frum told me that in her interviews with Margaret Thatcher and Jeanne Kirkpatrick, both of whom were feisty, they couldn't accept her. That powerful women couldn't accept being interviewed by a powerful woman.

JC: I think she's right. They wouldn't know her personally, wouldn't know her personal power, the enormous intellect and concentration. That would blow them away and they wouldn't like that. They would want more respect.

PM: Are there certain types of people you find hard to interview?

JC: Oh yes. There's one type of person I can't interview and that's a Junior League woman, a rich woman. I get so intimidated by the kind of poise rich women have, their lifestyle. It's so foreign to anything I know. They have my number. I cower and blush interviewing a rich woman and they patronize me. I get afraid I'm going to drop the teacup. I used to think it would change as I got older but I'm 60 now and I know I'm not going to get over it.

PM: Any final thoughts?

JC: The whole thing about interviewing is trust. I can't say enough about it. All you've got is your integrity as a journalist. If people can't be convinced they're dealing with an honorable person, you won't manage in the interview situation.

You know, I've interviewed crooks and murderers and welfare women and people who generally don't trust middle-class people and I don't have any problems. I don't find a barrier. I know they are lonely and that I am lonely and we have reams of material in common in our lives. I don't think anybody is a stranger to me. I've been everybody. I am everybody.

FEATURE INTERVIEW #2: Earl McRae

If anyone deserves to call what he does "the tricks of the trade," it's Earl McRae. Short and aggressive, McRae comes across as journalism's artful dodger, a cunning rascal who would go to almost any length to get what he's after. In McRae's case, the target is the psyche of the people he profiles. If he's to be judged solely on the end product rather than how he achieves it, then McRae is a tremendous success. His profiles of sports personalities such as boxer George Chuvalo, hockey tough guy Reggie Fleming and football pass receiver Hal Patterson are brilliant. Obsessed with finding out how they really tick, or more accurately how he thinks they tick, he employs tactics that are both ingenious and unorthodox. Listening to him hold court on the subject of interviewing, it struck me that he could get the same results without having to go to the lengths that he has.

PM: How much research do you do for a magazine story?

EM: As much as I can . . . before I speak to the person. Out of respect for them, because the more you know about them, the more likely they are to talk to you. I make all kinds of phone calls, to their parents, their brothers, their sisters, looking for anecdotes, looking for minutia. Where did they go to school, who were their teachers, who did they ever work for? I do this on the telephone.

PM: Can you give me an example?

EM: I did a piece on Mike Liut, the [former] St. Louis Blues goaltender, about four years ago. I knew he was from Woodbridge, Ontario, and I found out from the St. Louis front office that his father works in the Canadian Tire store [there]. So I called him up and said, "Mr. Liut, my name is Earl McRae from *Canadian Magazine* and I'm doing a cover story on your son Mike." I always say it's a cover story even if it's not or I don't know.

PM: Do you think that's fair?

EM: Yes, because it could be or it could not. There's a way of rationalizing it. So I play to their ego. "Cover story? That's great." So that works to my advantage. If it's not a cover story, so what. I ask Mr. Luit what kind of child Mike was, was he mischievous, who were his buddies, his teachers, who were his girlfriends . . . that sort of thing. Then I call those people up, and with them I'm always looking for anecdotes.

PM: Do you have any trouble getting them to talk? Do they get suspicious or defensive?

EM: Not often. I have a way of talking to them. I raise my voice a little, an octave, so I sound more ingenuous. I don't sound as threatening. And I agree with them and chuckle on the phone. You listen to them, gauge their personality by how they sound. If they sound kind of measured, then I'll sound that way too. I won't want to sound too goofy. Or if they're kind of, "Yeah, we was down at the beer parlor, eh!" I may talk that way a little too. Talk in the vernacular, deliberately screwing the language up myself, so as not to be patronizing. You've got to be a chameleon if you're an interviewer. I will adapt my personality to the personality of the person I'm interviewing, to his social level or his cultural level, because that makes him feel more comfortable.

Get them talking. Empathy is the key word in interviewing. That means at times you have to be a phony, you know, hypocritical, all those things. But the story is what matters. [You have] to open them up to get inside them.

PM: And did that work with Mike Liut?

EM: Yeah. I went out to Calgary, where the Blues were playing . . . we're walking downtown and my hands are in my pockets and we're chatting. But I'm always working. I'm opening him up, talking about Calgary to loosen him up a little, getting him to like me. I'm looking at how he walks, for little gestures, habits, how he dresses, listening for telling speech patterns. He thinks we're just walking along, but I'm looking for the small, telling details that illuminate the greater truth. Mike Liut has clickers, silver clickers on the bottom of his shoes, so he has a kind of image of himself.

[At one point I said] "You ever hear from Carol Mac-Gregor anymore?"

"What? Who the hell is Carol MacGregor?"

"The chick you took to the school prom that time. Remember the time Les Bannister didn't like you and came across and gave you a punch in the face and knocked you over the hood of the car?"

"How the hell did you know that?"

"Doesn't matter. Do you ever hear from her anymore? You were crazy about her." I got that from his mother. She [Carol] was the one love of his life. He was just smitten by her.

He stops in the middle of the street. "Are you FBI?" he asks. He was incredulous. Why? Because he was used to the same old questions and lousy research from sports writers and he was bored with it. But here's a guy who's gone to the trouble of learning a whole lot about him. It showed him I respected him. And he respected me for doing it.

PM: He didn't think it was an intrusion?

EM: Yes, he did at first. He said, "What right do you have to find out this stuff?" I said, "Mike, I am a journalist. This is what you do in my job. You're a good goaltender, Mike, because you work at it. What makes you one of the best in hockey is that you do a little more than other people. I'm the same in my job. I'm a little more innovative and creative."

"Oh. Yeah, I can see that. What else do you know? Did you speak to Carol? Do you have a phone number for her?"

My [note] pad is still not out. But now he's starting to talk about the past and he's opening right up about other things. And he's no longer talking to a journalist. He's talking to a friend. He's genuine and I'm genuine, but it's with calculation, a purpose. And finally I said, "Do you mind if I take my pad out?"

PM: Do you also prepare questions?

EM: I come in with pages of prepared questions. I have a basic set of questions that I ask everybody. And they're designed to open the person up and give me a greater dimension on them.

PM: Such as?

EM: If you couldn't be what you are, what would your second choice be? I asked George Chuvalo that and he said, "A great surgeon. Because they always get respect. Even when they're retired, people respect them and don't laugh at them." Are you superstitious? What makes you cry? When was the last time you cried? What do you admire the most about your mother and father? What do you admire the least about them? What is your greatest strength and weakness? If you could change one aspect of your character for the better, what would you change? All these are designed to give me a three-dimensional portrait of the person. . . . Interviewing is like swimming under water, holding your breath, it's so delicate at times. The slightest gesture, the slightest, can lose it. My philosophy basically is do whatever you have to do to elicit information within the confines of good taste.

The other thing is, I always go into someone's medicine cabinet. I always make a point of excusing myself and going to the can even if I don't have to. Often medicine cabinet doors make a little noise when you open them. So I'll flush the toilet at this point. Medicine cabinets are fascinating. Often they'll reveal a person's anxieties, ego. You might find Grecian Formula, maybe eyeshadow in a bachelor's apartment. Might belong to a girlfriend, who knows? But when you come out you might get the conversation around to ego, vanity, just to see if there's anything there.

[The subject of using non-existent credentials comes up.]

EM: I have done stories as a reporter where I have made up fictitious names and names of companies because fiction, the lie, is much less important than the truth I'm after. If that's the only way to get the information I need, if the public has a right to know this information, if the only way is to tell a lie to the person I'm talking to, then I will do it.

PM: It's a shaky philosophy though, isn't it?

EM: Not with me.

PM: How do you get people to open up?

EM: I always agree with them and I relate [what they're saying] to a situation in my own life. Or I make one up. . . . When [my article on George Chuvalo] came out . . . what had really bothered him was the bit I included where his father used to whip him in the basement and make him spend hours on his hands and knees on loose kernels of corn on the basement floor. He didn't like that in there.

PM: Did you ask him about that [during the interview]?

EM: Yeah. He said, "Where did you get that?" and I said, "From your father." He was furious because the article stripped him bare. I seemed so friendly, so dumb, like a buddy. What he didn't understand was that I'm working every second.

But the piece was totally accurate, insightful. Now we're friends. I brought him on my radio show. He said, "You know something? The piece wasn't that bad. My sister told me, 'That was you.' It's just that you hurt me." And I said, "George, that's my job. The truth sometimes hurts."

6

FOCUS: BROADCAST INTERVIEWS

So much of broadcast interviewing is style and image. Many broadcast interviewers believe that to be successful and taken seriously as defenders of the public's "right to know," they have to act tough. To these interviewers, badgering and constant interrupting are effective techniques to test the mettle of a guest.

While there are situations where these methods are called for, in the vast majority of cases far greater results will be achieved by creating an atmosphere in which people can speak comfortably, something they are not inclined to do if they feel under attack. Being a persistent, direct, and assertive interviewer is very different from being a quasi-police interrogator.

Robert MacNeil, of the *MacNeil/Lehrer News Hour*, exhorts students of the interview not to regard it as a hostile affair:

> Part of my approach is that this is not a prosecutorial situation. We're not here to embarrass people and make them look bad. We're here to elicit information and get them to share their views and knowledge with us and the people listening. Too many television interviewers see it as an opportunity to show off as much as to reveal or display the interviewee. That sort of prosecutorial style is largely empty and theatrical, but it makes the interviewer look very tough and it directs a lot of attention toward him. It's a show.
>
> I don't think it's hypocritical to establish some pleasant atmosphere between the two of you, some dignified and yet common human bond between you. . . . I think it's more productive. It's also much more ingratiating to the audience, so that you become a medium through which the guest talks to them, an

extension of their curiosity or creator of it. Not some kind of self-appointed prosecutor, which only contributes to the perception of arrogance and condescension in the media, perceptions which I'm afraid have a basis in fact.

Eric Malling of *the fifth estate* is known as a relentless, aggressive interviewer, but he too decries the need to flex his muscles unnecessarily:

I don't beat anybody up. I get them to tell their side of the story. I think they should be prepared to be consistent and if they start saying things that aren't true and I have information otherwise, I'm going to point it out, as forcefully as is required. But I don't beat anybody up and never have. And even if I wanted to, I wouldn't get away with it because the sympathy of the audience immediately goes to the person on the other side.

With an untruthful or evasive guest, cleverness, which works in conjunction with listening skills and intuition, is usually more productive than loud displays of outrage. In his autobiography *Close Encounters*, Mike Wallace of *60 Minutes* illustrates how he outfoxed John Connally, the former Governor of Texas, who was campaigning for the 1980 Democratic Presidential nomination:

In going through my research, I read that someone taped a remark Connally made in reference to the nuclear accident at Three Mile Island, which had occurred earlier that year. The comment, if true, could only be construed as a slur against the man who Connally and others believed would become the 1980 Democratic nominee — Ted Kennedy. When I asked him about it, his vexation flared into open anger:

MW: Governor, did you really say: "More people died at Chappaquiddick than at Three Mile Island?"

JC: No, I did not.

MW: You're sure?

JC: I'm positive.

MW: If I could show it to you on tape — [note that Wallace doesn't say he has it on tape]

JC: I don't care —

MW: Would you be surprised?

JC: I — no. If you did, you — you were taping something you shouldn't have been taping.

MW: Ho! Then — then —

JC: If you did, then you taped a private conversation. Sure, I've repeated it in our own home because it was a joke that's going around, and it's been on bumper stickers. I have never said it publicly. Never.

MW: Publicly.

JC: No sir. And if you taped it, you shouldn't have.

MW: Well, we didn't tape it —

JC: Okay.

MW: But it has been taped. And you said it.

More often than not, it's solid research that proves to be the backbone of tough interviewing. When the facts speak for themselves, as the saying goes, there's little need to yell and shout.

a. HANDLING THE TOUGH INTERVIEW

When you're pitted against a powerful and ruthless opponent, the interview can become an intimidating and frightening experience. To survive, or even hold your own, requires a strategy, one that may not be apparent without some study. Former Canadian Prime Minister Pierre Elliott Trudeau was considered the toughest person to tackle, for male interviewers anyway, during his 15 or so years in power. He had the intellect, quick mind, and vicious streak needed to terrify his opponents.

"For a feature interview, we always liked to send in two reporters," says Dave Roberts, who for many years produced *The House*, a CBC Radio program covering the week's events on Parliament Hill. "Because while he was busy knocking one of them off balance, which is what he tries to do, there's somebody else who's thinking about how to come back on him. It always helped to have a woman interview him because he was of an age where he treated men and women differently. He just was invariably more polite with women, less threatened, and would not try to be so aggressive with them."

With a complex person such as Trudeau, who came to hold the media in contempt, you may have to find a way to circumvent the automatic alarm system that goes off when a journalist approaches. Dan Turner, now with *The Citizen*, says he was able to do that when he covered national politics for Canadian Press and the Toronto *Star*. But it was not without its risky moments:

> . . . I found ways to get through to him. For instance, he would come out of the House and there would be a scrum around him, which he hated, and they'd all shove their mikes in his face or hurl two or three questions at him. And nine times out of ten he would storm right by them. I didn't know what would work with him but I thought, this doesn't. So I started to wait for him, out of range of the scrum because anyone could see that he hated crowds like that. And as he came by I'd say, "Excuse me, have you got a minute?" He responded terrifically to "Have you got a minute?"
>
> I enjoyed the mental jousting with him and I think he did likewise. So I would spend a lot of time preparing the wording and the tone of my questions for him. The tone was so important to him. He once smashed me on the shoulder when I used a different tone on him. I was standing in the lobby asking him a question about the temporary Wheat Reserves Act, which was, believe it or not, a big issue in 1970. The government had gone ahead and done something to finance a wheat storage system in the west that it didn't have Parliamentary approval for. I was with Canadian Press and I said, "So, you've broken the law." And bam!, he smacked me on the shoulder with his fist. It

didn't hurt, but you could tell he wanted to hit me harder. And he said, "Well, so you say." So I knew fairly early that that kind of approach would not work with him.

While Trudeau embodied the intimidating, slug-it-out style, the current Prime Minister, Brian Mulroney, presents a carefully crafted and controlled exterior that's hard to ruffle or break through. He is far more frustrating and difficult to interview than Trudeau. "Mulroney has mastered the 30-second clip," says Dave Roberts. "During the election campaign he was very well controlled by his media relations people. It was effective for him but frustrating for us. At one point the reporters covering the campaign had to refuse to get on the campaign bus [in order] to get a few minutes with him. He is extremely difficult to handle because it's hard to get anything but what he wants to give out."

b. EXPECT THE UNEXPECTED

No matter how prepared or experienced you are, every interview has the potential to throw you for a loop. When Helen Hutchinson was working for CBC Radio, an interviewee touched a nerve that left her speechless:

> I was cohosting *This Country In the Morning*, and we had done a five-part series on abortion. This was in 1971 and the right-to-lifers, who were just starting up, demanded equal time. So it was arranged that I'd tape an interview with Dr. Heather Morris, who represented the association.
>
> We were about 10 minutes in when I said, "Look, Dr. Morris, let me put it to you that if my 14-year-old teenage daughter is raped and impregnated and I bring her to you, what would you tell us, what would your counselling be?" And she said, "That it would be an ennobling experience for your daughter to have the child." My jaw dropped. That's the only time I've been rendered silent. How do you respond to that? I signalled the technician and we cut the interview.

And we ran it like that. She was pleased as punch with herself. She felt she had silenced me. I felt somewhat defeated and deflated.

When faced with an inarticulate or petrified guest, interviewers are inclined to panic. When you stare into eyes bulging with fear, or hear nothing but a barely audible grunt in reply to your brilliant opening question, it's not uncommon to experience an overwhelming desire to bail out as quickly as possible.

This type of interview may very well end in disaster, but should not be sloughed off as being without redemption. After all, the world is not composed only of glib media people who always have answers at their tongue tips. When Pierre Pascau was host of *Canada AM*, he decided to go the distance with a guest of limited elocution:

> I was interviewing a farmer from Regina who had seen a flying saucer land on his field. It was a remote interview — I was in Toronto and he was in Regina. He appeared on the screen and he looked like a farmer hillbilly. He was called Thud, so I said, "Farmer Thud, how are you?" Grunts. "What did you see?" Nothing. I said, "Didn't you see a flying saucer?" "Oh, that." I said, "What was it like?" "Well, like any flying saucer." It became comedy. It was hilarious, because it was like a game we were playing, me trying to make him speak and him refusing to speak. And the audience loved it.

c. CREATIVE QUESTIONING

To bring out the best in people, you have to spark their interest. It's creative questioning that separates the special and memorable interviews from the dull and predictable.

When radio broadcaster Stuart McLean interviewed actor Jack Lemmon, he wanted to avoid the routine. Lemmon was holed up in a hotel room and each media representative was allotted 15 minutes to get some quotes and go home. McLean figured that with limited time to try and make contact, he had to create a special occasion for the actor:

I spent three full days researching, reading magazines in the library, watching old films. I really felt I had to do something special because by the time I'd get to him in this media circus he'd be bored sick, so I knew I had to go in and blow his socks off. I researched his life as thoroughly as I could and I took all sorts of obscure references from his life, things that appeared in subordinate clauses done 20 years ago. I decided I wanted to play a word association game with him.

So I went into the hotel and he was looking bored as hell. And I said could I play word association with you and he said sure, it sounds like fun. And the words I used were words that I knew were important to him, that he would recognize — I can't remember them now — and after five or six he caught on to what I was doing. He was charmed and it ignited all sorts of anecdotes from him in a very lively and interested way. Because for radio, if the person doesn't speak with some enthusiasm, the interview has a lot less chance of being a success.

You should always be on the watch for ways to make an interview more than just run-of-the-mill. A few years ago I was covering an international festival of Welsh music and culture for a documentary on the natural singing ability of the Welsh. I was told that two first cousins who had not seen each other since 1913 had been reunited. They were in their late sixties or early seventies, full of energy and blessed with the lyrical Welsh tongue. After interviewing the cousins for several minutes I asked if they would sing together. It took some mild cajoling but they soon relented. To my pleasure, they found a tune and not only sang it with perfect pitch, but broke into natural harmony. More than any interview or narration, this moment captured the essence of the documentary.

"Conversation is the art of never appearing a bore," said nineteenth century French writer Guy de Maupassant, "of knowing how to say everything interestingly, to entertain no matter what, to be charming with nothing at all." To stimulate the intellect of an illustrious and articulate guest, you have to entice him or her with challenging or provocative questions. Part of that ability is natural, but more than anything it's developed through hard slogging — by thorough research and preparation and the constant studying of the art of conversation.

The process of becoming a good conversationalist escalates as you relax and learn how to be yourself on-air. That can take time. "It took me a season and a half of doing daily television shows before I was able to forget about the lights, lose my fear of dead air and of not having my next question," says Peter Desbarats of his days as a TV interviewer in Montreal. "I remember distinctly it was in the middle of my second season before I was actually listening and starting to have a real conversation in the studio."

The conversion from stiltedness to a more natural style also requires a certain letting go, having the confidence to make mistakes. In *Sweaty Palms: The Neglected Art of Being Interviewed*, author H. Anthony Medley relates how holding back can affect novices and professionals in all endeavors:

> Mean Joe Greene played defensive tackle for the Super Bowl champion Pittsburgh Steelers. The first half of the 1976 football season was a bad one for him. He played subpar football and the Steelers suffered, losing several games in a row.
>
> Suddenly things turned around. Greene became the player he had been, and the Steelers, who had lost four of their first five games, won eleven in a row, allowing only twenty-eight points in their next nine games. What had caused the turnaround? "I was trying too hard not to make mistakes," Greene said. "In the past, I never gave a damn about mistakes. I used to play about 70% by design and 30% freelance. I'd take a chance now and then."
>
> Once Greene forgot about himself and how he was performing, he resumed playing at the caliber he had achieved in the past. It was the thinking about what he wanted to do and worrying about mistakes that caused him to make the mistakes he was worrying about.

Vicki Gabereau has developed into one of the top radio personalities in Canada thanks to her original, sassy style of interviewing. From her Vancouver studio, the host of *Gabereau* interviews authors, actors and other major entertainment figures with her unique brand of sharp-tongued yet highly informed banter. Success for Gabereau came with the realization that she had to release herself from the restraints of how the typical CBC host should sound and let her personality make or break her:

> I started out doing straight, standard interviews. But I found that that wasn't what I was particularly good at. And so, as I got more confident, I learned you're only paid as much as you are willing to be brave. And the braver you get the more notice you get. Not that that's my particular interest. But if you are prepared to go out on a limb and make a fool of yourself, if you get to do it long enough and you get it under control, you can take all the chances you want.

> It's scary at first, letting your real self come out, but if that's what got you where you are in the first place, it only makes sense that that's what's going to keep you there. I'm not sure it can happen before you've reached a stage where you've mastered the basics, to a reasonable extent, anyway. But it's always there, under the surface, trying to get out, so it's worth the gamble to see what happens if it does.

d. SENSITIVE SUBJECTS

Sensitive topics are always tough to handle. There is a tendency to be either too sentimental — oohing and aahing at the guest's relevations — or too cold and unfeeling. These responses may come from discomfort with the subject matter, or from not knowing how you're "supposed" to react to someone's story about rape, torture, a debilitating disease, or whatever issue is being discussed. And quite unpredictably, these kinds of interviews can have profound emotional impact, hitting you much harder than you might expect. This is what happened to hard-boiled Tom Snyder on the now-defunct *Tomorrow* show on NBC:

We had a woman on a couple of years ago in L.A. who had been raped by a man in San Francisco known as "Stinky." She went through the whole experience of being violated with her three-year-old child outside the door, knocking on the locked bedroom door. And she touched me. For that hour, I was ashamed to be a male, I was just ashamed of my gender, that a man had done this to a woman, violated her in such a fashion, raped her. And that show haunted me for a long time.

What the guest and audience need from the interviewer is to let the person tell the story without editorializing. You don't have to prove that you're outraged, offended, or sympathetic by stating so after every traumatic statement. That can be accomplished more with the tone of your voice and the support, through listening and discipline, that you offer the speaker. Instead of jumping in the second there's a pause, you must be disciplined enough to let the silences exist. Someone who's reliving a horrible experience needs time to reflect or gather composure, and the audience needs time to integrate their feelings.

The silence itself is part of the answer, as freelance radio broadcaster Marie-Andrée Michaux saw so clearly during an interview several years ago:

I was interviewing a French painter. He was about 70 or 75 years old. I don't remember his name. He had come with his wife to the studio. He was a man who had suffered terribly during the war and for whom painting was a sort of therapy. And at a certain point we got to the topic of suffering and there was a huge silence. And then his answer came from far away — his wife was crying, and this was live on-air.

It was very delicate but at the same time it was very real. I'm sure the silence — which didn't scare me — said more to the listeners than any words he could have used.

e. POINTERS ON BROADCAST INTERVIEWS

From the experience of professional interviewers it's possible to cull some tips to keep in mind:

(a) Most broadcast interviewers advise against talking to a guest about the specific details of an interview just prior to the start of recording. "It's extremely important that you chat people up," says Helen Hutchinson, "but only on neutral issues, to establish some relationship with them. If you discuss the actual interview, often they won't repeat their great answers because they've just told them to you; or that horrible phrase, 'As I was telling you earlier,' comes up."

(b) Make sure your guest knows what the interview is about. Because there's a fear of the guest launching into answers before the tape is rolling, what often happens is that no information of any kind is given before the interview. That information can be provided without having to go through a dry run.

"I was always very careful to make sure that people understood exactly what was going to happen," says Peter Desbarats:

> I didn't believe in sneaking up on someone. I know that those kinds of techniques are used at times when nothing else will work, and I have perhaps done that on occasion. But I feel that even if you are going to do a tough interview, it's better to be as above board as possible. I found most people would respond to that. If they understood why you were going to be tough and they felt they could hold their own, then it really made a very good interview because I could relax and not worry beyond the actual content. If someone felt extremely nervous, I might give a detailed explanation of what the interview was going to be like.

(c) If a pre-recorded interview is not going well, take some action to try and salvage it. "I'll stop the camera," says Jim Reed of W5:

> If they're running on at the mouth or they won't let me get in and ask any questions, I'll speak to them

directly. "This is verbiage and if you don't stop, it's going to end up on the cutting room floor." It really depends on who it is and how you think they'll take it.

If someone seems really nervous at the outset, sometimes what I'll do is turn the camera around and ask the questions with the camera on me and go through the interview. Then I'll do it over again with the camera on the guest and often the answers are far better the second time.

It's more tricky to rescue a live interview that's failing. Often there's no other choice than to speak bluntly, as Tom Snyder did with a famous but taciturn guest:

> I asked [Joseph E. Levine] how he got from being a man who ran a restaurant in Boston to one of the most successful independent movie producers. What were the things that happened along the way? Well, Levine looked at me and said, "I was in a movie studio in Astoria in 1939 and somebody showed me a script and the rest is history." And he stopped. And I looked at him and he looked at me and I looked at my watch and said, "You know, Joe, we have 42 minutes to go here, and if you could give me a little bit of this history as we go along, it would be very, very helpful."

(d) If you're just after specific clips, especially for non-confrontational stories, be upfront with the guest about what you need. Take the time to explain how the interview will fit in and the length of clip you're likely to run. The day I interviewed Patrick Watson, he was expecting a TV news crew to arrive to get his opinions on a pornography issue. "I just need to take a couple of minutes to figure out what my 30-second clip should be," he said, acknowledging that that was the most airtime he was likely to get. Rather than pretending that an incredibly unspontaneous system is actually spontaneous, give the guest a chance to rehearse and perform — when appropriate — just as you do.

(e) Interviewing more than one guest at the same time creates some logistical, but manageable problems. The challenge is to keep the conversation flowing so that it isn't dominated by one or two speakers, while others aren't heard from at all. That can be accomplished by directing questions to specific people, or asking them to add to, or comment on, a point made by someone else.

If you're interviewing a group of people, particularly out-of-studio, there is the potential that several will talk at the same time, overriding each other. Your ear must be attuned to that to see if it has resulted in an important point being missed. When that's the case, try to calm the hubbub down, then ask the question again.

Especially for radio, it's often hard to identify who is speaking when a collage of voices is heard. To compensate, you can address the person by name at the beginning of your questions.

(f) For "person-on-the-street" interviews, the key is to understand what it's like to be accosted by a stranger with a microphone and/or camera and asked your opinion on a subject right out of the blue. "You have to keep them talking," says Larry Zolf, a self-proclaimed master of the "streeter." "The trick is to hang in there, talk to them, make them laugh, get some response out of them. Don't just ask one question and run away. Who can come up with a great response just like that?"

As a veteran of street interviews, I agree, and I offer the following additional suggestions:

- As with any story, have an angle you want to pursue.

- Ask yourself before going out: what would I answer to the questions I've selected? Is the topic something that people will be able to think of answers to on the spot?

- Have more than one question, because you need to develop a conversation.

- It's the why of the answer that's more important than the initial response. If you ask, "Should priests have to be celibate?" it's not yes or no that's interesting, it's the reasons for the opinion.

167

- If it's a complex topic, you may have to supply some information in the preamble to your question to help the person understand the context. "As you may be aware, the federal government plans to implement a minimum tax of 24% so that rich Canadians can't avoid paying tax through the use of tax loopholes. Do you support such a measure? Why?"

- Humor is your best friend. To hold someone's interest on the street, you get the best results if you entertain them. Wit and self-deprecating humor will keep someone talking, and will help ease their nervousness about saying something foolish on the spur of the moment.

(g) For editing purposes, especially in feature reports or documentaries, it's preferable if a guest begins an answer with the wording of the question. For example, if you ask, "What were the worst moments of your ordeal?" and the person replies, "Coping with the snakes," the answer makes no sense without the question. That means narration has to be written or some other means found to make the answer sound logical. If you ask the guest to repeat your question at the beginning of every answer — "The worst thing about my ordeal was the snakes . . ." — it can be incredibly helpful. Although the guest may forget, it's surprising how many are able and willing to cooperate.

(h) The post-interview period should be as important as the pre-interview. Too often in this business, once the interview is over, the guests are yesterday's news. "There can be a great letdown afterwards," says Warner Troyer. "Some of them feel exploited or manipulated. The person needs some contact after the seduction of the interview."

Peter Desbarats agrees. "Quite often it's a real high for the person, who is not used to performing. And like any performer coming out of a performance they are quite exhilarated and they want to talk about it and I think you should try and respond to that. You shouldn't act as if you just used them for the interview and as soon as the business is over you're no longer interested in them. I think that's really insulting and it really turns people off."

f. RADIO SHOPTALK

While professional technicians work with you on out-of-studio shoots for TV, radio interviewers are usually on their own. Talent as a reporter does not necessarily bring automatic technical expertise. Many don't really know their equipment and use it incorrectly. Stuart McLean talks about microphone techniques and other tips for radio interviewers:

First of all, it's important to sit very close to a guest so you don't have an outstretched arm holding a microphone for any length of time, because it's agony and makes it very difficult to concentrate.

I mike people about an inch or two just below their mouth and off to the side, so that their p's don't pop and they don't see the microphone. It might sound crazy but if you put a microphone below a person's chin they can't see it and it doesn't bother them as much.

I often touch people during interviews to give them cues. If I ask them a question and they are about to give an answer and I'm not finished my question, I'll just put my hand on their arm to show them I'm not finished. It's important that they don't begin their answer until my microphone is in position. (It's also important to mike yourself at the same pitch as the guest if your questions are going to be heard in the interview.)

I'll ask the same question several times if the first answer isn't insightful enough or does not have the information I know is required. A technique I use, to get them to tell a story for me, is to ad lib an intro and then stop talking and have them pick it up from there. For example, I'll say, "The day Fred Boggs was shot there were hundreds of witnesses. One witness, the closest, thought . . ." and I'll stop and shove the microphone in the person's face and he'll say, "Well, I thought . . ." I've never had anybody rebel or say I was putting words in their mouth because I'm not. I choose the words they've already used and all I'm doing is focussing their minds toward it. I always finish that sentence on an upbeat and they always answer in a fabulous tone.

g. SCRUMS

Named after the shoving, pushing, and grunting scrummage in a rugby match, the journalistic scrum is one of the least dignified aspects of the profession. The scene is all too familiar: a politician is surrounded by a small unit of reporters, a collar of microphones circling his neck. Questions are fired from every direction, with some answered, others ignored, and little of substance being said.

Dave Roberts, who worked on Parliament Hill for about a decade, dislikes them intensely:

> I hate scrums. They're unprofessional, ridiculous, and loathesome. But if it's the only chance you have of getting to the guy, you have to do it. With a lot of politicians these days, there's no other time you can get to question them.
>
> On a normal day outside the House of Commons it's not unusual to have 60 people in a scrum. There would be 15 camera crews, which is 30 people, and about the same number of reporters. Sometimes scrums don't even get started because the politician is surrounded by people who don't ask questions. I've seen where the guy's had to ask for a question because there was no reporter of any description in sight. People have been physically hurt from falling, arms broken or twisted. Those camera guys are big because of the weight they have to carry.
>
> By its very nature, it's not something that's going to go on very long because it's extremely uncomfortable, physically uncomfortable for everyone. Right away the politician has control of the timing of it and all he has to do is pick the questions he wants to answer. The questions are coming in four or five at a time and he only hears the ones he wants to answer. They've learned to look at the camera, so you could be

170

behind the politician and he doesn't even look at you, he thinks so little of you as he answers. It's a desperate attempt to get something quotable on the air. And that's what it is, desperation, and it suits the politician's needs perfectly. He's in control of everything and then when he's through he can just say thanks very much.

FEATURE INTERVIEW #1: Barbara Frum

We met in a small cafe in Toronto's fashionable Yorkville area on a damp afternoon. Despite having one of the most recognizable faces in Canada, because of her position as host of *The Journal,* CBC-TV's nightly public affairs program, we weren't interrupted during the three hours we spent together.

I spent six months trying to convince Frum to agree to an interview, but she was most reluctant to discuss the profession at which she is such an expert. She explained that she disliked the coldness of a transcript, because the absence of tone removed so much of the meaning from what was said. She finally relented, however, and talked with energy and eloquence about interviewing. "I don't care if I'm understood," she said, "I just don't want to be misunderstood."

PM: Do you still enjoy interviewing?

BF: I love it. I can't think of anything about it that I don't enjoy. It's a special kind of interviewing that I do now. *The Journal* has particular requirements. And although I enjoy that, there is no doubt that at times I yearn to be much more wide-ranging, be able to go much deeper into things. Some of the things that I particularly care about — for example, why people do the things they do — really can't be handled in a seven-minute *Journal* interview. I miss that very much.

Increasingly, I'm glad to say, we are booking more guests like Robertson Davies, Geraldine Ferraro, Anthony

Burgess, or even Dr. Ruth, for longer and more wide-ranging conversation. And we are doing some big-scale productions like our AIDS forum and our preview of the Geneva arms talks. They offer a chance to take more chances, which is what makes interviewing such a risky occupation, and which I love to do. . . .

PM: How close to actual time on air is the amount of [taping] time you have with guests?

BF: Close, very close. I think of my role as an on-air editor more than an on-air interviewer. I'm an editor because I know the time I've got and I know the story I have to get. And I have to get that story in an economical way.

PM: It's a very subjective thing, determining what you go after. What's the process you undertake?

BF: What I do is, I hear out my producers and then I work by myself. If there's guidance that I find useful, I use it. If not, then I'm on my own. Then I go through a process that I don't think I could define. I think that's the part that's inexplicable.

PM: Do you write out questions in point form or actual form?

BF: In actual form. On radio, I used to be able to write them in point form because I was able to keep on writing as the interview proceeded. But on television, you can't do that. . . .

PM: Do you plot out the counterpoint of the interview — the "if-I-say-this-he'll-say-that" plan?

BF: No, not at all. I never do that and I never did that. I think if you overplot your counter moves, you end up reading the questions off the paper. In a way it's funny, because I work so hard at writing all this stuff out in longhand and often I never look at the paper again. I suspect that I don't have to work as hard as I do. . . . When I write things out longhand, I'm hearing myself ask the question and hearing if it sounds right. And there is something about seeing it that allows me to hear it. . . .

I try very hard not to stuff data into questions. When I was young, it struck me that most interviewers are really showing off. The question that begins, "As we all know . . ." — well, we don't all know, Mac, that's why you're there asking questions. . . . You're there every night, the guest is there only once. Let's hear what they've got to say.

PM: When you mentioned hearing your questions, it made me think of tone. I don't think enough interviewers pay attention to the tone of their own voice and the tone of the person being interviewed. Are you concerned about tone?

BF: Very. Very. Different tones are appropriate in different interviews, though some guests can spoil your battle plan. You will not be able to stay calm with every guest, no matter how much you're determined to stay calm. You're going to quaver. But I find that you may quaver on the first question, then you get over it.

PM: I think there's a belief that if one's tone is very nervous the other person will respond to that nervousness.

BF: Absolutely. And a lot of interviewing is actually just releasing someone to speak, just making it possible for them to speak. Either because they are nervous by temperament or because they don't want to speak.

Another thing I do is I always tell people where I'm going. I always tell them the purpose of the interview and what I want to achieve, ahead of time. And if it's going to be a hostile interview, I always tell them that. But I don't say, "This is going to be a hostile interview." I say, "You've done something or you believe something that a lot of people don't agree with, and I want to discuss it with you."

PM: Do you find that makes it easier to talk to them?

173

BF: I think it's only fair. I hate ambushes. First of all, I think they're unwise. They turn the audience against you, and they rarely work. Because a person that's ambushed will not undress for you as you think. He will react to the ambush instead of the question. And the audience may misconstrue his reaction. . . .

PM: A lot of people feel abused by the system —

BF: That's why a lot of people at *The Journal* tease me that I'm out on the street too much. But I feel that I have to allow people I'm talking to a chance to get back at me. How else am I going to know how they're reacting, how they're feeling, if they can't react? If you are insulated and never outside, people can't say to you, "You were unfair," or, "I found our encounter very off-putting." And I am perhaps one of the few people at *The Journal* that knows how off-putting the process can be. I can hear it in the way they [guests] breathe. I can tell just by listening to their breathing, before we even start.

PM: You're very sensitive to breathing?

BF: I am very sensitive to sounds. And I suspect that one of the reasons they hired me is because I could reach people over a telephone line. I could really hear what they were doing and feeling. . . .

PM: [Does] a guest pick up a tension in your breathing?

BF: Not so much that, because I think you've got to be very tense to do the job. That's one of the requirements. You have to be very, very acute and keen and alert. You have to be at a point of high, nervous energy to work. If you're relaxed you don't care about anything.

PM: I agree. You have to have it. But at the same time —

BF: — you have to control it. If you're not up, the guest doesn't feel your energy. And then they will not be in the right mood to talk to you. So a lot of what I have to do, before we start, is to talk until we reach a state where we can talk to each other and the audience will get something out of it.

PM: You would raise their energy level?

BF: Yes. And I am usually very blunt about it. I'll even kibitz, if necessary.

PM: How do you do it?

BF: I just sort of joke, about myself and about them. It's part of getting somebody ready to talk to you. To give them some idea of who you are and what you're like. Also, to show them that you have some appreciation of who they are and what they are. . . . It's a gift, an interview is a gift. People don't have to give it to you. Sometimes if they're too exhausted, they're just too played out, you can hear it. I just kibitz around till I wake them up. . . .

I have to project myself as a human being. And that's where flirting fits in [earlier we had briefly alluded to flirting, which she said she never does]. I never think of myself as either a woman or a female. I never think about that. I'm not that interested in gender differences. I mean, I don't know why anybody would rely on it [flirting]. It's so cheap.

PM: It's amazing the number of male interviewers who describe the interview as a seduction.

BF: They are the flirts. Men are the worst flirts of all. Absolutely. I don't see it that way at all. I don't care if anybody likes me — I don't want them to dislike me, but they don't have to be in love with me.

PM: You're self-described in Susan Crean's book (*Newsworthy: The Lives of Media Women*) as being "aggressive."

BF: That word is so loaded that I wish I never had to use it again. I would like "aggressive" to mean clear, straightforward, direct, open, honest. Even bold — I think that's okay. It tends to be used when people mean someone who has an edge of hostility and is harsh and wants something. I just want to be clear and straightforward. I want to liberate. I want to be so comfortable with myself that the guest doesn't have to worry about me. "I'm all right. How are you?"

PM: There are interviewers who have a different goal, which is that their needs, consciously or unconsciously, are very strong.

BF: I think one of the big divides is whether or not the interviewer needs to be liked or admired. . . . They really want that guest to be knocked out by them. So they seduce, because they don't want to decide how they feel until they find out if the other person is enthralled with them. Then they'll decide if they like the other person. So it starts with themselves instead of with the guest. . . .

PM: Many interviewers talk about the interview in a patient/therapist context. Do you see it that way?

BF: No, I don't. There's a belief that under hypnosis people will do and say the most extraordinary things that they would never do if they were conscious or alert. That's just a myth. It's the same myth with interviewing. People will tell you what they are prepared to tell you and really nothing more. And if you get something wonderful, chances are it was possible to do so. Your therapy doesn't undo the valve — they wanted to talk. They were waiting for someone to come in and ask the question. The most exquisite praise you can get is, "I'm so glad you asked me that. No one has ever asked me that."

PM: What do you think about the "How do you feel" question?

BF: It's too simple and it contains too much. It asks for too much revelation in too boring and unresourceful a way. The interviewer has to earn the answer. You have to deserve a good answer because you've put a lot of thought into the subject, because you care about the person. . . . You usually get what you deserve with a question like that, which is lather. You can take the most thoughtful person in the world and destroy the interview because the question doesn't stimulate them enough. Doesn't mobilize them enough to think and feel. Feelings are great, but you have to ask them a question that allows them to answer. . . . I'm very interested in [how things really are]. I can't stand things that are less interesting than the truth. Truth is always more various and more contradictory than it seems. And that complexity is what I'm interested in. . . . I have to watch that I'm not so interested in a topic that I can't squeeze all my questions in.

PM: To the time allotted?

BF: Yeah. And I'm always frustrated because sometimes people say the most extraordinary things when you're finished. When you ask, do I miss radio, actually I miss print, because it was through print that I discovered how much fun talk is. But radio is still the best for interviews, as far as I'm concerned.

PM: Most people are afraid of going past a certain point, going too deep.

BF: I think that's worth talking about, because that gets back to aggressiveness. I'm afraid of real things, like death, dying, suffering, and all those things that everybody is afraid of, but I'm not afraid of much else. I'm not afraid of what you'll say or what I'll say. That's why, when you ask me if I write down my counterthrusts — if that fails, ask this — I say no. Tough luck. Skydive. Here we go. I'm trying to think of situations that really make me afraid and they're very few.

PM: But you are dealing with people who are often very much afraid —

BF: But I don't want them to be afraid, so they are not afraid for very long.

PM: Do you think that's true — that you can calm them down just because you're not afraid?

BF: Absolutely. I'm not suggesting that because I talk to them, they're no longer afraid. I'm not a healer. But I don't want them to be afraid.

This touches on not caring what other people think of you, because if you do it makes you too afraid. If you're afraid to appear stupid, I think that's the most unnerving fear for most journalists. They're even afraid in a group not to be part of that group. Pack journalism is one of the biggest sins of our game. When journalists operate in a pack, what starts to work is their fear of each other, of not being in the right mindset on a topic that the pack has decided on.

PM: Do you think you're lied to on a fairly regular basis?

BF: I'm having trouble with the word "lie." You're talking to me. I'm not telling you everything I think. You're not telling me everything you're thinking. People couldn't live if they were totally frank. Civilized life couldn't go on. . . . I think you rarely get what you and I would classify as raw truths. And the more power someone has — and therefore the more power to protect — the less you get. The more you've got to protect, the more closed, in a way, your communication is. You cannot expect someone on radio or television to tell you the raw truth very often, unless they had an extraordinary experience which they want to share. But they're not lying. They're just not telling how it really is. . . . You have to be realistic about what you can get, but still keep striving. You have to remember who you're working for. You're working for people who are going to turn on their set tonight and want to know. You are their agent. You're the one who's asking the questions that they want asked. And that's why you write out your questions in longhand, and you do it so carefully because, even knowing the limits, you mustn't concentrate on the limits. I must concentrate on what has to be asked. It's very challenging, very intellectually stimulating.

FEATURE INTERVIEW #2: Peter Gzowski

Anyone who has listened to Peter Gzowski, as host of *This Country in the Morning,* or its present successor, *Morningside,* on CBC Radio, knows that something special happens when Gzowski speaks into a studio microphone. More than any of his peers, Gzowski has mastered the ability to be intimate with his radio audience, projecting a combination of warmth and interest that makes each listener feel that "Peter" is there just with him, two friends finding out what makes Canada and the world tick.

We spoke in his small, cluttered office at *Morningside,* after one of his three-hour stints in the studio, a demanding amount of time on-air for a daily program that does mostly live material.

PM: Are you primarily an instinctive interviewer or do you follow the "green" most of the time? ("Green" is the term for the research and suggested questions prepared by the producer who arranged the interview, written on six-part green paper.)

PG: I'm not sure I'd like to choose one over the other. My instinct is to say that I'm often instinctive. But there are two things that qualify that: one is that those instincts have been shaped and honed over 30 years of whatever we call this craft; and the other is that the spontaneity occurs long before the item goes on-air. As I come in each morning, I start shaping pieces in my head, or I start thinking of questions. And contrary to what you might think, I have been known to follow a green exactly as it is, because a lot of thought has gone into it. But when I get to the green, I go through it all and block it out in my mind. I think it through — what will he say there, at what point do I ask this? I think about things like pace, and surprise at the top, and try to reach a nice conclusion and tie it all together. I try to shape a piece, an interview, much the way I would try to shape a magazine article. The lead-sublead-explanation-tailpiece pattern comes into effect when I think of a radio interview.

Now that I'm a "veteran" interviewer, I'm much more comfortable with my instincts than when I first began. I have learned how to be more natural, and learned not to be nearly as afraid of my human instincts as my instincts told me to at the beginning. But that's an intellectual process. I will actually feel myself getting emotional or getting silly or getting embarrassed or getting stupid. And intellectually will give myself that license. I mean that actually happens in my head. I think, "You're sounding like a dope." And then I say, "But it's helping the piece. The listener is getting something out of this guy that he wouldn't have got if you weren't being a dope. So go ahead, be a dope." I actually think about that.

PM: Be vulnerable, expose yourself.

PG: Right. That's one of the tricks you have in your arsenal. It's really, "I'll show you mine if you show me yours." If you exhibit a little bit of your own discomfort or lack of knowledge or something, it shows through. It makes the interview subject feel more comfortable about letting his show through. I do that all the time.

I don't mind ever thinking out loud or appearing to think out loud myself. Many things are contagious in an interview situation. You can even control your subject's speech pattern, control the speed with which he'll talk. When you talk fast, most people will talk fast in response. And vice versa. You can speed up a slow talker by giving him staccato questions. That's contagious. . . .

PM: It's a very difficult mix of the contrived and the spontaneous, the real and the unreal.

PG: I'm probably making it sound much more complicated than it is, and much simpler than it is. I mean, essentially what you do is you go and ask a bunch of questions and you get a bunch of answers. . . .

PM: But it's a lot more complex than that. . . .

PG: Well, I would distrust anybody who denied [that]. I'm sure there are people who are simply good interviewers.

They're curious, they're pretty bright, they're polite, they're not so hooked on their own egos that they feel the interview is a place to demonstrate their ego. But it's also a learned skill. I know people who meet those characteristics but aren't somehow good interviewers.

PM: How did you learn?

PG: I don't know. [When I joined radio] I had nothing going at that time except 15 years in newspapers and magazines. And a lot of that was as an editor. I always hated asking questions for print, you know. I am not a good investigative reporter.

PM: Why do you think that is?

PG: I don't know. I'm shy. I look over my celebrated book [*The Game of Our Lives*] on the Edmonton Oilers [hockey team], and I think of all the things I would like to know about the guys I wrote about, as a reader and when I was writing it. I'd like to talk to Jari Kurri about his childhood in Finland. How it was different from Mark Messier's childhood in St. Albert, Alberta. But I could never screw up the courage to ask this 19-year-old kid about that. I thought it was none of my business.

PM: I know that feeling. Almost that you're intruding.

PG: Absolutely. I don't like being intruded upon myself and I don't like intruding. The only feeling of relief I got was from one of my great heroes, A. J. Liebling. It was in a biography about him, and he said he hated what he called the direct question. I hate to ask somebody, "How old are you?" If I really care, I should know that. It seems to me a rude question. "Where were you born?" [I don't like asking it] unless I can phrase it in some interesting way.

PM: You're much more comfortable in radio than you were in print, in terms of imposing and so on, I imagine.

PG: Well, I always figure if a guy is coming into my radio studio, it changes the whole rules of the game. I'm not in his space anymore. I'm not imposing on him. He's come in and said, in effect, "Here's 15 minutes of my life, do as you will with me within the common bounds of good taste and topicality." I'm not an abrasive interviewer and it's very interesting when I step out of my usual affable, aw shucks role. It really pisses people off. . . . But when I turn nasty, openly nasty, it usually shows. I'm very careful about it now. I mean, I say tough things, but I couch them in the nicest, suckiest language I can.

PM: Why is that?

PG: Well, it's to maintain a kind of consistency to the program. We have a continuing success in having people on this program and wanting to come back. Even though they know they'll be asked tough questions, they're asked politely. I think that good manners are essential to the way I work on radio. You have a certain place in the listener's mind. . . . You've got to be the same person all the time.

Years ago, on *This Country In The Morning*, a prominent Quebec labor leader said that he understood the motivations of the Palestinian guys who killed the Israeli athletes in the Munich Olympics. I shouted at him (I can't remember what I said), and the listeners almost totally condemned me for that. I learned a huge lesson from that, that any kind of bullying, no matter how antagonistic you feel, transfers the listener's sympathy away from you to the bullied guy. . . .

PM: Have the listeners shaped you?

PG: I have learned a great deal from the mail. I also listen to myself all the time. On days when we have tape, I listen and rail against my bad habits. I listen to an awful lot of radio and watch a lot of television. I'm always watching interviewers, seeing what they do. Is this too soft, that too hard, how did they get that great answer?

I learned a very simple lesson watching Patrick Watson years ago. I've never talked to him about it, but I'm sure he knows it. And it's the principle that most broadcast guests, as much as nature, abhor a vacuum. If you shut up, the guest will keep talking and often you'll get more by shutting up than asking a question. Just stare at the guy, particularly when he's said something stupid. He'll expand on it. But you watch the younger, other kind of interviewers. They'll think, "Ah, this is my opening, I'll go in and show what a smart digger I am." You clam the guy up. People are too afraid of silence, the way they're afraid of their own instincts. They think, I cannot let this moment go by without filling it with a word. Well, you can fill it with a silence.

PM: Did you come to a point, an epiphany perhaps or a slow understanding, of what worked on radio and and why you were so good at it?

PG: I know one simple fact about radio that transcends all the other understandings that I have. "People" don't listen to radio, "persons" listen to radio. Individuals. The radio is the most intimate medium left to mankind, except perhaps for books, which you can read curled up in a chair. You listen when you are by yourself. You listen in your car, and usually turn it off if there's someone else with you; when you're in bed; when you're doing your chores; when you're in between things. It's a solitary act. So the radio listener is a person you speak to singly. I challenge people to hear me say, "*All* of you out there. *Most* of your letters. *Everyone* within the sound of my voice." I never say that. I will say, "There's a guy right now driving between Swift Current and Moose Jaw who's just gone off the side of the road because of what you [the guest] just said." What that is in my mind is a message to the listener that there are other listeners. It's amazing the number of times I have said that little playful thing and it has been the truth. I'll get a letter saying, "I was driving. . . ." Once you have that understanding, it begins to color much of what you do. Because radio is not show business.

PM: What it is it, then?

PG: Well, radio is a telephone. You don't do show biz on the telephone. You don't phone up your mother and do an act for her. You phone her up and tell her what's on your mind. So that colors all of my langauge and the way I speak. It's an intimate thing, an intimate relationship between me and the listener. I also fight the word "interview." I think it establishes a formality to the listener. Except I find "conversation" a little affected. I don't know what else. "Encounter"?

PM: There are times when a guest is opening up and you know if you take them one layer deeper, they are going to break down, cry, maybe reveal things that are very intimate. Do you stop them, protect them, at a certain point?

PG: The line I draw is where I feel embarrassed myself. If I am embarrassed, then my assumption is, so is the listener. If I sense the current is flowing toward my own discomfort, I'll try to divert that current.

PM: Do you feel you have a fairly middle-of-the-road discomfort line? Are there areas [on-air] that you don't like going into?

PG: Well, I think maybe one of my weaknesses in this job is that I have a high embarrassment threshold. I'm easily embarrassed.... I tend to think of my grandmother listening, so I sort of want to say, "I don't think we should talk about that now." I'm one of the most foul-mouthed people I know, and I don't pretend that I'm not foul-mouthed, but I don't swear on the radio. I'm really careful about that. To me it's good manners, respect for the audience. But it may be a weakness. You might get better ratings or there may be unsatisfied curiosity. I know there are producers here who think, I wish he'd go after that farther. I think we're both right. This is the way I do it, and I cannot bring myself to go through that barrier. I wouldn't pay the price for whatever I'd get back from it.

PM: One of the curious things I've discovered is that many interviewers, particularly broadcast interviewers, are shy. I wonder why that is? . . .

PG: I would say that shyness, a really essential desire to keep your own privacy, is what allows you to sit there for three hours a day and let other peoples' egos go flipping out all over the place. People say to me, you reveal so much about yourself on the radio. I do and I don't. I reveal facts and I reveal emotion. But I'm secretive. I'm a private person. And most of the people who say they know me very well, from the radio, can't answer very many private questions about me. . . . [Canadian author] W. O. Mitchell told me: "You're such a ham, you're such an actor. Every day you go out there and play your role." Well, that's very hard for me to admit to myself because my role is in constructing a person who is someone I can tolerate. So, is that reality or is it role-playing? That's a philosophical question and I'm not sure how helpful it is to pursue it. Because there are obviously a lot of contrivances, beginning with the very simple fact of the man who does not swear. This is obviously not the real guy, okay? People say, "Are you really interested in all those things?" Well, patently not. . . . But I'm also paid a lot of money to supply the answers to the person who is interested. It's my job at that point to say, what does that person want to know?. . . So, that is demonstratively contrived. But there are other moments that I treasure on radio that have been about as close to real as radio can be.

PM: Can you give an example?

PG: Oh, it happens all the time. I did a piece last week with Harrison Salisbury, who's written a terrific book about America, *Vietnam Reconsidered*. And every question I asked, I would have asked him if I'd run into him at a cocktail party. And most of the good pieces are like that. "God, I've got a chance to talk to this person. Here's what I'd like to know." And at that point, all the 30 years of training, discipline, shaping of instincts, and knowing that you're old enough and free enough to be yourself, all come together. That's the joy. . . . I would pay to come down and do [those interviews], almost in the literal sense.

7

FOCUS: PRINT INTERVIEWS

While the primary task of a print interviewer is to obtain information and quotes — especially for newspaper articles — the scope of the role goes far beyond that vital but narrow dimension.

"You're always looking for irony, symbolism, some kind of setting or context for a print interview. The quotes themselves aren't usually enough," says freelance writer Earl McRae:

> I was at the Canadian Tennis Championships four years ago. Bjorn Borg injured his ankle and withdrew. He refused to give any interviews following his withdrawal. I bluffed my way past two security guards . . . by being aggressive and walking around like I owned the place . . . and was able to get into the players' trailer.
>
> Borg is over in the corner with his head in his hands, sitting in front of his cubicle. He's got an ice-pack on his leg and he's in pain. There are other players sitting around. None of them ask me who I am. The fact I got past two security people means I'm somebody. These players are on the road and they don't know if Wednesday is Saturday, never mind who I am.
>
> I walk over to Borg, hands in my pocket, affecting the casual look. And I said, "Is it bad?" He looked up. "Yeah, it's bad. But what really bothers me is that the U.S. Open is next week. That's what I want to win. I just use the Canadian Open as a warmup. It doesn't mean anything to me. In fact, it means nothing to any of the players."
>
> This is great stuff, but I'm also on the lookout for irony, something to help give the story a context.

Then I notice there's a poster on the wall behind Borg, showing him holding a big jar of Gatorade with a big smile on his face. And the caption says, "For perfect health and happiness, drink Gatorade." And beneath this poster, there's Borg looking anything but healthy and happy. Beautiful irony. And I'm listening to the sounds in the room, the smells, sights, trying to convey and capture the total feeling of the situation with all my senses working full out. I went into the can and wrote down verbatim what he had said and all my impressions of the room. Then I walked out and said, "Well, Bjorn, all the best." He said, 'Yeah, t'anks man, t'anks.' "

"You are always on the alert for moments of revelation," says Richard Gwyn, "and they often don't come in the interview itself." The role of the interviewer, therefore, demands that you be the keenest of observers, absorbing every detail. You must watch scenes unfold with the critical eye of a theater director, noting the secondary characters and the action around them, listening for natural dialogue or anything else that could add color, texture, synthesis, irony, or pathos to elevate your story beyond the ordinary.

Don Obe, a writer, editor, and former chairman of the School of Journalism at Ryerson Polytechnical Institute in Toronto calls this "writing out of the ethos."

You incorporate everything into your work. You look at how people are sitting. Listen for a favorite expression you can use to define their character. Gestures, actions, whatever's happening in and around them — you absorb it all because it's all part of the story.

Jimmy Breslin [a reporter with the New York *Daily News*] started this years ago. Say there was a new conference at city hall. Nobody's notebook or pencil came out until the person being interviewed started talking. What Breslin did was start recording everything that was happening before that: the nervous PR man testing the microphone, what the reporters were saying, what the room looked like. And he put it all what the room looked like. And he put it all into context, to produce a story of what the conference was really about.

Daily deadlines restrict many newspaper interviewers from doing more than gathering quotes and collecting or confirming information, often over the telephone. However, when it's possible — and it's imperative for magazine writing — the aim is to expand the interview beyond the formal sit-down session. With some writers, such as Roy MacGregor, this approach can be taken to extremes:

> For most of the profiles I do, the least important interview is the subject himself. I find that I'm doing it only out of courtesy because the person expects it. So I go through with it, but I'm virtually asleep. I do pay attention, and I end up using quotes from it, but it's nothing compared to the work I've done before then: all the interviews with people who know the subject, all the time I've spent with the subject, in different settings, watching him interact with others. That's where the real interviewing can take place, in just knowing how to spend time with people.

Before succumbing to the bright lights of television, Tom Alderman was a magazine writer who epitomized the non-interviewing style of interviewing:

> You get the best quotes for magazines by just hanging out, a couple of guys, hands in pockets, no cameras or microphones, just talking as friends. I don't think of it in terms of interviews. I just like to have conversations, have them forget I'm a journalist. I usually didn't take notes. This may not be for everybody, but I always thought that if I couldn't remember what was said, it wasn't worth remembering. People would say to me, "Hey, how come you're not taking notes?" They'd get nervous. And I'd say, "Because you're worried I'll misquote you?" "Yeah." And I'd tell them, "If you come up with a good quote, it will be burned into my memory. I'll not forget it. If I get it wrong, sue me."

Among the innumerable advantages of "hanging out" is the opportunity to see behind the masks that people usually — and understandably — wear during the "official" interview. "It's far better if you can see a person in action with somebody else," says freelancer David Lees. "They may still be acting, but if they're acting with somebody who shows up in their daily life, at least the person they're reacting with is going to anchor them and pull them down to some level of credibility. But with a stranger, they have some license to be whoever and whatever they think they should be."

a. CASING THE JOINT

Whether you're hanging around or sitting across a desk from the interviewee, train your senses to notice physical descriptions and other details in the environment. You can take actual notes then or at a later date, if it isn't appropriate to do so on the spot. If that's the case, make a distinct effort to "burn the information into your memory," as Tom Alderman says. If you're making notes, take down as much information as possible, no matter how insignificant it may seem at the time. It's uncanny how a minor detail that didn't seem important can turn out to be of the utmost value at the time of writing.

If you interview an actress in her home, for example, try to get overall impression of the style of furniture and decor. Look for unique or highly personal ornaments, paintings, and other art objects. If you see a painting, for instance, that catches your interest, try to get the name of the painting and the artist. It may be of value to ask the actress directly not just for the information, but why she likes it. Frequently this can lead to revealing areas of discussion.

Look carefully at how the person is dressed, both for future description and to see if it tells you anything that could be of value during the interview. I remember meeting a powerful and wealthy member of the arts community who, to my surprise, was dressed in cheap clothes in need of repair with holes in the soles of both his shoes. I knew

189

that his father had been a down-and-out alcoholic and I felt there must be a connection between that and the way the man presented himself. That synthesis — which proved accurate — gave me confidence to explore his relationship with his father, a delicate but worthwhile pursuit that yielded fascinating insights about his character.

Minor characters can play important supporting roles in your narrative. Don't focus solely on the person you're going to see. Talk to secretaries, doormen, taxi drivers, spouses — anyone who might be able to shade the guest or story in a different hue. For a profile on hockey analyst and former coach Don Cherry for *TV Guide*, among those I spoke to was his tailor, Marty Alsemgeest from Toronto. Cherry is known for his flamboyant taste in suits, and Alsemgeest willingly provided colorful quotes to illustrate that point. Cherry, he said, has "an athletic seat," (size 48), and the "task of camouflaging it" put his talents to the test. Another challenge, he said, was to keep the wardrobe selections toned down. "Don likes to wear velvet suits," he said, "but I tell him, 'Don't do it. They make you look like a musical dancer.'"

b. THE EXTRA EFFORT

It is quite appropriate to interview someone several times over the course of preparing a story. "I will talk to the person initially, get things sorted out, go off and speak to a whole lot of other people, then maybe come back two or three times to the person I'm writing about," says Don Obe.

Linked to this approach is a tenet of journalism I hold with great conviction: if you make extra effort, especially if you have a gut reaction that something is missing or not quite right, there will be many benefits. If you don't follow that instinct, you're playing with fire. Roy MacGregor agrees. "It's that extra phone call, that last-minute bit of research or checking that can often make a piece really work."

For a *Financial Post* magazine feature on Cindy Soini, a paraplegic who has a full-time job, runs a thriving consulting service to accident victims on the side, and is the mother of two young children, I did several lengthy interviews with her over many months of research. Although I had mounds of material and had actually started writing, I knew that I was missing a scene to really tie the story together, so I called and arranged for a final chat.

It proved to be the right choice. The day we met, she had just returned from a one-day trip to Milwaukee, where she had consulted with a client who had been disabled when a van struck her on a Toronto street. Soini's day had begun at 6:45 a.m., when she drove herself to the airport, and finished after midnight when she returned to her home in Markham, Ontario. She had communicated with her client through the painstaking process of using an alphabet board (her speech had been affected because of the accident) and dealt with the problems of getting around when her wheelchair was left behind by the airline during a stopover in Detroit.

Her day made a perfect lead-in to the story. By taking the time to revisit her, I was presented with a perfect framework from which the article flowed effortlessly. There's no guarantee this extra initiative will pay off every time. But it seems to happen often enough to make it well worth the effort.

c. GUIDELINES FOR YOUR INTERVIEW

The following pointers will be especially useful for print interviews:

(a) Establish how much time has been set aside for the interview. Something to remember is that busy people like to be told the interview will be brief, but most interviews last longer than expected. First of all, if the experience is interesting, the guest will want it to keep it going. "When I interviewed [former Prime Minister] Trudeau in 1978 [for *Grits: An Intimate Portrait of the Liberal Party*] I was briefed to the eyeballs," says Christina McCall. "He was so intellectually demanding. My questions interested him a lot, though, and he waved his staff away several times so that we could continue." In the same vein, time in an interview passes more quickly than guests imagine, especially if it's an enjoyable session.

(b) Begin the interview at the pace you feel is appropriate. In most cases this will mean easing into it slowly. You might start with some general, nonthreatening questions, allowing the person both to warm up and become more comfortable with you. But there are exceptions. If time is short, or you sense that you need to capture the guest's attention immediately, you may want to go directly to your key areas of discussion.

(c) Don't bore people. Too many print interviewers don't work hard enough at making conversation flow and sparkle. If you enervate your guest, he or she is not going to perform at top level.

(d) Unless there's a reason to be evasive, tell people what you know about the story. "I always let them in on what I've figured out so far," says David Lees. "It's also useful to tell them what you're trying to say because often they will respond to that point. Often you'll get a good lead-in quote from doing that, as they pick up the story directly from the point you mention. The more they know, the more they'll work with you. People are always compulsively helpful to interviewers. They pine to help you."

(e) Worth reiterating, because it's of vital importance, is don't ever say you understand a specific point or general explanation unless you do. The cost when you sit down to compose your story far outweighs any embarrassment or loss of power you feel if you admit your confusion to your guest. If you sense the guest is irritated about your lack of understanding, it may help to remind the person that, first, it's difficult to grasp a new topic the first time it's explained; second, it's better to be accurate than get the facts wrong; and, third, reporters can't be experts on every subject they cover. Many interviewees presume, because they are specialists in their field, that anyone sent to talk with them should be also.

(f) It is essential to check information. Don't assume that, because there are quotation marks around a statement, it's a fact.

(g) Get people to provide specific details, such as what they ate for breakfast on the fateful day, what they were wearing, and the exact date an event happened. But if they're engrossed in the telling of their story, don't keep interrupting to pick away at their memory.

"When you're asking people to remember, the first thing is just to let them remember," says Barbara Sears, who has done innumerable interviews as author Pierre Berton's researcher. "And never argue with them over questions of fact. That's irrelevant. The important thing is what their impressions and feelings are, what stayed with them over that period of time, even if you know a fact they're stating isn't accurate. You have other sources for checking dates and that sort of thing."

If you note the specific points that are missing as you go along, you can raise them at the end of the interview or during a follow-up conversation.

(h) There's rarely the need for a print interview to become confrontational. "The dumbest thing a print interviewer can do is argue with the person you're interviewing," says Don Obe. "Ninety percent of what you get you're not going to quote anyway, so it's best just to keep the person talking."

(i) When you hear a piece of bombshell information, try not to give away your resulting ecstasy. "When someone says something that signals 'major story' and that you had no idea about, I get this feeling of Oh my God, I'd better not change the expression on my face, I'd better not let him know that he just told me something that's the key to my story," says Judy Nyman of the *Toronto Star*. "And it's very difficult for me, from that point on, to remain cool and calm and conduct the interview in a normal manner, as if the earth had not just stood still. Which it had."

(j) If you doubt the trustworthiness of what an interviewee is saying, start off by raising significant points you've already researched.

"When Jack Anderson, the widely-known Washington columnist, wants to check a damaging bit of information with the person involved, he always begins by asking a question to which he already knows the answer," says Hugh Sherwood in *The Art of the Journalistic Interview*. "Then, if the man starts to give an answer that is not in accordance with the facts, Anderson says something like, 'Now wait a minute. Court testimony indicates . . .' or, 'I have a document here that says. . . .' He finds this approach usually throws the interviewee off stride and thus makes him more vulnerable to probing questions."

(k) Be on guard against being deluded by someone who is a smooth talker or attractive person, as Judy Nyman explains:

> One of the most obvious things that I think both junior and senior reporters forget is that there are two sides to every story. I don't think it's fair to print a story — and it could be the biggest story in the world — if you don't try to get the other person's side. But it's very easy if somebody is very glib or a good talker or very personable. They can suck you in so easily and make you believe their side so that before you've even gone to interview the other person, you've already got a bias. You already know how you're going to write that story.

(l) There will be times when politeness and patience aren't the best ways to deal with a guest. It depends on the circumstances, but as Tim Heald, an English freelance journalist and author, says, "You have to know when to stand up for your rights." Heald describes an interview he did with Gary Player, the South African golfer, while working in Canada for the now-defunct *Weekend* magazine:

> I wanted to interview Player for about 20 minutes for our "Day in the Life" column, but I hadn't been able to make contact with him despite considerable effort. So I went down to a tournament and came up to him after the eighteenth hole. He'd had a bad round.
>
> I introduced myself and he was quite ratty and said, "How would you like it if you'd just finished an important round of golf and were feeling low and some berk [slang for "idiot"] comes up and asks you for an interview?"
>
> And I said, "Look, if you don't want to do the interview, that's fine. I don't care. But just for your

information, I've tried everything to get in touch with you and to arrange this beforehand but I failed. You didn't reply to my telephone calls or messages. I have been as professional as I know how. I apologize for disturbing you at what seems a bad time, but this is the only time I can see doing it. If you don't want to do it you only have to say so and I'll go away." After I'd done my spiel, he said, "I'm sorry and I understand. Come into the locker room and we'll do it there." And we had a perfectly agreeable time. Generally speaking, if people are gratuitously hostile, I find I fold my tent and go home.

(m) A way of getting information, especially when interviewing people in law enforcement, is to offer information in return. "The police are very cautious in how they deal with you," says Wade Rowland, who was a crime reporter for the Toronto *Telegram* for many years. "It takes a long time to build up a good relationship. Relationships are built up on swapping information. You tell them something they don't know and they tell you something you don't know.

(n) Be aware that many of the people you interview are sophisticated and know how to handle the media.

(o) If you're going to ask a tough question, make sure you can follow through. During an interview with Paul Anka, John Keyes of *TV Guide* tried to but failed:

He was a scary man, a martinet with the people around him. When I was interviewing him about the old days, about when he wrote "Diana," there was no problem. He loved it. But I wanted to talk to him about the stories that he has mob connections. I said, "Since you have talked about your delight in writing 'My Way' for Sinatra, and the words Sinatra and Vegas connote the mob to the average reader, how do you feel when your career has that aura to it?"

He said, "It's ridiculous" — said it with reptilian speed. When he snapped the word "ridiculous" in a low voice, it was like a gun cocked. I changed the topic.

(p) Journalism can be a very judgmental profession, often to the detriment of people who don't fit our values or worldview. "We judge all the time," says Don Obe. "We judge on the basis of style, demeanor, the kind of place someone lives in. George Cohon [the President of McDonald's Canada] has a toilet seat that's a facsimile of a Big Mac. Now that's not my taste, but I have to look beyond that and not immediately categorize him. You have to respond beyond your own taste."

(q) If you are doing a series of interviews, start with the easiest, most general ones first, then move to the more specific, tougher ones as you go along.

d. USING QUOTES

"On the rare occasions when I didn't really like a person, I quoted them verbatim," says Jay Scott, the film reviewer for the *Globe and Mail*. "There's nothing crueller you can do. I started off using a tape recorder for my interviews because I was so concerned with accuracy. But I soon discovered that if you used exactly what people said almost anyone would sound illiterate. You have to clean it up and that can include making a few changes to make sure what you've quoted makes sense."

Jay Scott is right. Most of the time it's impossible and unkind to quote with 100% accuracy. Natural speech is rarely grammatically perfect, completely coherent, or presented in a logical, easy-to-follow order. So, for a story to make sense, you nearly always have to do some minor tinkering, slightly changing what people say for the benefit of the readers and the person quoted. Eric Malling of *the fifth estate* agreed to an interview for this book on the understanding that "You don't quote me verbatim. I don't mind being taped and I'm happy to talk to you," he said, "but quite frankly I ask in return that you clean up the grammar and so on because I don't want to be quoted the way I talk."

An unclear verbatim quote is worse than a slightly altered quote that says what you know the person intended to get across. That doesn't mean you can make drastic changes to suit your own needs, but there is some leeway for the sake of clarity.

There are, however, occasions when the exact wording is crucial, no matter how jumbled. A politician's statement in a scrum, for instance, concerning a major policy decision, should not be changed to make it more intelligible. If the language is imprecise, that can reflect his or her state of mind on the issue. In addition, what is said is going to be broadcast and quoted in other publications. It isn't right for the politician's words to come out in different versions, depending on the source. In fact, a good rule is that unless there's a reason, don't alter the quote. Legal considerations aside, people have the right to expect they'll be represented faithfully when quoted. Sometimes the only way to accomplish that objective, though, is to improve upon the original:

"I think you can quote accurately without quoting verbatim," says Wade Rowland:

> If you're quoting a Polish immigrant, you don't quote him in broken English. You clean it up to some extent, which is all that happens if you use a notebook and reconstruct later on. There's more to accuracy than literal accuracy. It's the essential accuracy. If you're saying exactly what the person wants to say sometimes you can help them say it a little better. It takes a lot of experience and training and you can't play fast and loose with other people's quotes and information. You have to handle it responsibly, but it can be done well.

e. PUTTING IT TOGETHER

Once the interviewing for a story is completed, there remains the question of what to do with the material afterwards. Each writer will develop his or her own state of the art, but some general principles apply to most cases:

(a) Work from an outline, no matter the length of your story. It can vary from a few hastily sketched points to a detailed, extensively planned blueprint. At the very least, the outline should include the major points you want to cover and the order in which they're likely to appear. At best, it could be almost like a rough draft, indicating not just how the story will unfold, but what quotes will be needed in the various sections.

Preparing an outline forces you to get organized, a major step that many inexperienced writers pass by. Faced with a mass of research and pages of quotes, you can become entangled by indecision and confusion, not knowing how to start or where to proceed.

(b) If you're having trouble getting started, spend some time just thinking about the story, perhaps jotting down some points as you go along. One of the most common problems for writers is the lack of a clear understanding of what the story is really about. Unless you can answer that, the writing is likely going to be troubled. Ask yourself: What am I trying to say? What's the main thesis? What would someone conclude after finishing reading? Mulling over these questions helps to reveal whatever structural and philosophical weaknesses exist.

"Journalism is basically storytelling and every story has a beginning, middle, and an end," says Don Obe. If you keep that simple, though telling, definition in mind, it will help in the preparation of an outline. After you've determined what your piece is about, consider three broad yet key questions. Where does this story begin? What major points have to be included for the story to be complete? How do I end?

(c) Organize and become familiar with your quotes. It's worth the time, especially for long articles, to develop a system that will make it easy to find quotes on different issues and subjects.

If, for example, you have ten interviews, each two or three typewritten pages long, it's helpful to go through them annotating and underlining what quotes you anticipate using. I use different colored markers to highlight certain topics. I make notes in the margins indicating what each quote is about. For example, with every interview for this book where listening skills were mentioned, I'd write "listening" beside the quote in large print, making it easy to find all the listening quotes when I scanned my notes. One of the ancillary benefits of going through your notes this way is that you get to know and remember your quotes.

(d) Although transcribing tapes is time-consuming and physically draining, do it yourself if possible. First of all, it's very expensive to hire someone else. Second, you can do it faster, for you can edit as you listen, leaving out sections you know will never be used. And last, as you transcribe, you learn and remember a great deal, especially if the interviews took place some time ago.

To speed up the process, I use my own hieroglyphics, abbreviating words as much as possible. I leave room in the left margin for notes, and a lot of white space between paragraphs so that it's easy to find the material when I look over a page.

If you are working from notes, you can go through the same procedures, underlining and marking where everything is located. Another method is to transfer the notes into different form, perhaps typing them or writing them by hand in a more organized fashion. Some people find using small cards very useful.

(e) For a question-and-answer format, the interview can be rearranged so that the final version does not even resemble the chronology of the original. Quotes from two or more answers can be linked together, as long as it doesn't distort or misrepresent what the speaker intended to say.

In *The Craft of Interviewing*, John Brady described how former *Playboy* editor Murray Fisher works on a transcript:

> When Fisher sits down to edit an interview transcript, he begins by drawing a line across the page whenever he senses a jarring change of subject. He then re-arranges the pieces of the interview, taping sections together so that one subject leads inexorably to the next. This usually means that long sheets of paper are hanging from Fisher's office walls. "For my Fidel Castro interview, which later ran as a book," he recalls, "my entire office was wallpapered with long sheets, which I then had to abstract into a manuscript of

perhaps 20 or 30 columns that seemed to be a piece, not merely a series of excerpts."

Fisher sifts an interview transcript into three categories: "A material, which must be used; B material, which is desirable but not absolutely necessary; and C material, which is expendable, to be used only if necessary for transition or filler." The best interviews have only A and B material; but any transcript undergoes "a tremendous amount of processing, distillation, orchestration" before it is publishable.

FEATURE INTERVIEW: George Plimpton

My interview with George Plimpton was not a success. I had prepared a series of questions that took for granted that he perceived interviewing to be as fascinating and complex an art as I consider it to be. I was interested in this man who has given dilettantism and participatory journalism a good name for many reasons. I figured that Plimpton, journalist, author, amateur athlete *extraordinaire*, and editor of *The Paris Review* (the respected literary magazine that has published interviews with authors about their craft since the early fifties), would have much to say about the art of extracting information from willing or reluctant mouths. When I discovered the opposite, I experienced the panic that races through you when your most careful plans go out the window and you must scramble to readjust.

PM: How much preparation do you do?

GP: I read everything I can about the person beforehand. I don't trust myself enough, particularly if it's about somebody's work I don't know all that well, to go in and hope it's going to work out. You have to do your homework, otherwise the interviewee becomes impatient and the exercise becomes a waste of time. If he has to supply the information that you should have found out as the interviewer, it makes him less agreeable and therefore the interview more formal and stilted.

PM: Do you actually write out the specific wording of questions?

GP: The important thing about doing an interview is that you have to have some idea of what the final form is going to look like. There has to be some peg, something that you are aiming toward that is going to be divulged, to try and make it as artistic as possible.

For example, with [novelist] Joseph Heller, we did an interview with him for *The Paris Review* in which the most interesting part of his writing is how his books begin. They begin with a sentence that somehow pops into his mind quite unexpectedly. And the whole novel unravels from this one sentence.... When you learn something like that, there is your peg for the interview.

[After a few questions concerning techniques of interviewing, which Plimpton found perplexing, the following exchange:]

PM: Some people do it [use techniques to make a guest comfortable] very deliberately. Almost like a psychologist's technique.

GP: Well, I don't know anything about those people.

PM: Do you think it's a very dangerous thing to get into?

GP: You make interviewing sound like a science or a great art. I don't think it is.

The great thing in interviewing is editing. The interesting interviews are those that are worked on and shifted around and have a type of literary quality of their own. Anybody can turn on a machine and ask somebody something, whether they think of themselves as doctors or psychologists or detectives. That is not anywhere near as important to me as what they do with the stuff they finally come out with. If they do their homework and ask intelligent questions and the interviewee is somewhat at ease, then they have the raw material to do something with.

If you start thinking about the relationship you have with the interviewee, other than simply to extract information, I guess one would go crazy. Body language and the rest of it — to hell with it. I just think that's wasting a lot of time.

I can't imagine someone wanting to become an interviewer. What is an interviewer anyway? Is there a new bloc called interviewers? They should be called reporters. Every reporter does interviews. I hate to think there's a whole class of people — "What does that guy do?" "Well, he's an interviewer."

PM: You don't think somebody can learn the specific skill?

GP: And only write in terms of interviews? Read Elizabeth Hardwick in the *New York Times Review of Books*. She talks at length about people who begin to think that the tape machine, with its volumes and volumes of stuff pouring out of little twirling tapes, is literature. It's not.

PM: What would it be then?

GP: Garbage. Or grist, to be turned into something [Truman Capote's] *In Cold Blood* is a remarkable book. It's full of interviews. It was done in an interview format and then the interviews were turned into a work of art. [Mailer's] *The Executioner's Song*, which got a Pulitzer Prize, I don't consider a work of art. And nor do I think it is possible to turn interviews into a work of art.

[My book] *Edie*, which I worked on with a girl named Jean Stein, has a great deal of artificial work in it — called editing.

PM: When you piece an interview together, do you work from a transcript?

GP: I usually try to put the transcript in reasonable English first and take out the ellipses and the er's and the sentences that are repeated. Then I work it around the way one fiddles when putting together a puzzle, trying to find a beginning and an end, trying to arrange it so that things are not brought up in the interview that you don't know until later on.

PM: Is it fair to make changes in the questions asked? To make the interviewer look smarter?

GP: No, no, not smarter. Just to make the question a little easier for the reader to understand.

PM: Do you do the same with the answer?

GP: You have to be more careful with the answer. First of all, you show the interview to the person. I always do, after it has been done. And as long as you don't change the meaning, you can change the words a little bit.

PM: And you give people full review of it?

GP: Yes. Why not?

PM: You don't think they'll try and soften it, make themselves look better?

GP: I don't mind that. I'm not talking about the sort of interview you are talking about. I'm talking about writers putting down what they want to express about their own work. It seems to me that if you can get more explicit about something, then you should welcome that. Some people realize that when they speak and it's transcribed, it doesn't come out as they might have hoped. Very often it sounds strangled and wordy. They often don't find the exact words they want to use.

With *Paris Review* interviews, what we are trying to do is extract information on the craft of writing. It doesn't matter a damn bit of difference whether you get exactly how they said it. The important thing is to get what *they* want to say about it. So very often the interviews are carefully reworked by either the interviewee or by the interviewer, because you can get the most awful jumble of junk — even from the most extraordinary people. The tape recorder is not always an accurate dispenser of what one has to say.

PM: Where would the inaccuracy come in?

GP: In inflection. And, as I say, many people when asked a question don't answer it as well as they might with a pencil and pad of paper.

PM: Many journalists are fearful of presenting questions and getting prepared responses, especially after the fact. They feel some code that once an answer has been given, that's it.

GP: That's hopeless to me. That's ridiculous. It's the idea that the interviewer feels he has the goods and here it is down on tape and that's the truth, and why should he give it back to the guy who said it for a second chance. It's an unholy attitude, I think. And false. There are a hundred ways of saying the same sentence. The meaning is changed by inflection. Sometimes when you speak you get so carried away with yourself that you forget to make the salient points for your arguments.

For example, I just finished an interview with Elizabeth Hardwick. She talks about the first lines in her books and I sent the thing back to her and said, "Elizabeth, can you add something here to make this just a bit more clear?" She was delighted to do so. I mean, who are we trying to fool? If you send the interview to someone, particularly the direct quotes, they will come back much better.

8
FINAL NOTES

a. CHOOSING A LOCATION

Since the birth of formal journalism, interviews have taken place in every location imaginable, from the exotic to the mundane. Until the advent of television, the emphasis was on choosing the proper time and place, a restriction that placed many locations off limits. But thanks largely to television's need for pictures of events as they happen, society has become accustomed to the ritual of questions being asked in operation rooms, spacecraft, battle zones, or wherever journalist and subject have come together.

Despite this freedom, the vast majority of interviews, for practical reasons, are held in two or three typical sites: an office, a home, on the street, or in a restaurant or bar. The choice of location should not be made unthinkingly, however, for it can play an integral part in the story and can have a bearing on how you interact with the guest. While TV journalists are trained to select an appropriate backdrop — more to meet their visual requirements than for other factors such as the comfort of an interviewee — print and radio reporters tend to pay less attention to this important detail. Often there is no alternative, especially if you have a deadline to meet. Then you get to wherever the person is available. But when there is an option, it's worth considering which site is the most advantageous:

(a) Decide what kind of atmosphere would be most conducive to achieve your goals. If you want your guest to relax and speak informally, a social setting, such as the person's home or a restaurant, may be preferable to an office (although some public figures resent being asked to use their homes, choosing to keep their public and private lives separate). But for an interview you anticipate will be confrontational, a person's home might not be the most suitable choice. A heated conversation in a person's home

205

might seem like a violation of social rules — "I invited you into my house and you turn around and attack me" — and could afford the interviewee a chance to deflect the discussion away from the subject and toward your motives.

(b) If you opt for a restaurant, be advised that certain logistical problems can result. David Gritten, an entertainment writer with the *Los Angeles Times*, avoids them whenever possible:

> First of all, the food gets in the way. Either the person wants to eat and not talk, or talks so much he or she doesn't eat the food. Meanwhile, you are eating away feeling guilty that you're finished and the person has barely started. And it's too noisy. When you play back the tape, you have the waiter saying, "And our specials for tonight are marinated scallops . . ." over some important piece of dialogue. And if you interview stars or famous people, as I often do in Hollywood, there are constant interruptions at the table which destroy the continuity of any conversation taking place.

There are several tactics to offset these legitimate concerns. If you are working with a tape recorder, make sure it's placed where it can pick up the guest's voice clearly. A prior sound check helps to determine this. If there is loud, overhead music, this can interfere with the clarity of the recording. I have, on occasion, asked for the music to be turned down, and been obliged. You can also ask for a quiet table, explaining it's because you're conducting an interview. I did this in a cafe in the Ritz Carleton Hotel in Montreal for an interview with actress Céline Lomez. Not only did the waiter comply, he directed other guests to tables away from us, protecting our "privacy." Or, it may be advisable to leave the interview until after the meal, using the time beforehand to get to know each other. If something important is raised, take written notes as you go along.

Although chatting between bites can often help the guest to forget that it's an interview, a restaurant does not automatically swing the atmospheric pendulum in your favor. When John Keyes of *TV Guide* interviewed Tom Selleck, Keyes felt the meeting place arranged by the star seemed chosen to keep him at a distance and in his place:

> We met at an exclusive restaurant overlooking the ocean, the kind of stuffy place where the tablecloth was so starched you could hurt somebody if you threw it across the room. The feeling in the restaurant was very similar to how he was: cold and formal. I don't think getting him to open up is easy at any time, but it was a real struggle in that atmosphere. The interview went along boringly, which wasn't surprising considering where we were.

(c) Interviews in bars or over drinks can also help to break down some of the formal barriers and, as the guest becomes more relaxed, yield valuable information that otherwise might not have come out. If the guest becomes drunk, however, mark what is said with an asterisk and check its veracity thoroughly. While sometimes it may be the best decision to match your guest drink-for-drink, keep in mind that as lips become looser, *both* parties tend to reveal themselves. Your objective may be to sniff out the real story, but your guest's may be to find out your intentions. David Anderson, a professor of law at the University of Texas, warns that, with the frequency of litigation against journalists these days, you must be extremely cautious about what you say and to whom:

> As any lawyer would say to you, do not ever engage in any loose talk. Be careful not to use terms like "nail" or "out to get" somebody. It's a natural human emotion to feel that way with certain stories, but those are words and phrases that every journalist should purge from his vocabulary. If you're drinking, even with someone you feel safe confiding in, the chances of that kind of talk slipping out increases. That's not to say don't interview in bars, but be aware that the stakes can be very high these days, with million-dollar

lawsuits in some cases. And slip-ups don't just happen in bars. You have to be on your guard at all times if a story is in any way contentious. Your motives can have a great bearing in any ensuing litigation.

(d) It has become voguish with certain issues, such as elections or major sporting events, to search for "the pulse of the average citizen" in bars and pubs. While the bar scene can provide a handy stock of usually cooperative guests, it does not necessarily represent much of a cross section of the population. If the demographics of the people whose opinions you want match those of the patrons in the drinking spot, then it's bonanza time. Otherwise, it may be necessary to go farther afield to solicit a genuine sampling.

(e) When you're doing "streeters" or any interviews that involve a sampling of opinions, take the demographics of the interview location into account. For example, streeters about attitudes toward welfare may produce drastically different results in a fashionable part of town than in a low-rent area.

(f) There is much to be gained, especially for feature articles, by doing the interview at the guest's home. "That's my preference for talking to people," says David Gritten who used to work for *People* magazine:

> You can tell an incredible amount about somebody by the place in which they live. It reveals so much, leads to so many more areas of questioning that you might not have thought of if you had done the interview elsewhere. My interview with Fred Astaire, which was one of the best interviews I've ever done, was an example of that. He lives in a house in the hills above Beverly Hills, where Mary Pickford and Douglas Fairbanks used to live. It's not a huge house but it's wonderful. The funny thing about it is that there are no old photographs, nothing in the way of memorabilia. Just a couple of Oscars in a sort of drawing room. There was no indication that this was a famous person, that he had had a wonderful career in the past. He said he didn't like to dwell on the past, he lived in

the present, which for an 80-year-old man was remarkable. The setting told that better than anything I could have drawn out of the interview.

Earl McRae's favorite place to do interviews is in a car. "It's great for asking tough questions, because there are a lot of distractions — the traffic, things to see — and those can help to lessen the impact of what is being said. It doesn't seem like an interview if you're talking away, struggling with traffic, looking at the scenic views. People open up more in cars . . . and it also provides good material for description in the article. When you're moving around, things happen, scenes change, there are a lot of benefits."

(g) Look for opportunities to diverge from the expected formal setting. Jay Scott of the *Globe and Mail* met actress Maureen Stapleton in the Hilton coffee shop in St. Petersburg, Florida, to talk about her role in the film *Reds*:

> She had been interviewed to death about Warren Beatty and the film and I could tell she was close to being talked out. We began talking about *Trivial Pursuit*, which she is a freak about, and from there we wound up playing a complicated word game called *Botticelli*. We played that for about an hour and a half, during which time she talked a lot about Warren Beatty and *Reds*. And then she said, "Well I guess we should begin the interview now." And I said, "There's no need. I have what I need. I've been taking some notes quietly." And she said, "My God, that was painless!"

Just as eating hath charms to calm the savage (or nervous) guest, so too does walking or moving around. "For magazines, what you're looking for is anecdote and a feeling of character through dialogue and action," says Pierre Berton:

> I once interviewed Christopher Morley, who was then a very well-known American novelist and on the board of the Book of the Month Club. He said to me, "I feel the coefficient of civilization in any given city is in

its second-hand book stores." And I said, "Then why don't you and I go around and look." And the interview was conducted in second-hand stores as we opened books and talked about them. That's what I call the walking interview or the moving interview.

(h) The location for an out-of-studio radio interview should not be chosen haphazardly. The background sound is the equivalent of television's visuals and can add or detract from the interview.

For an interview in an office complex, decide whether you want a relatively noiseless room or one with specific background sounds. The former is extremely difficult to find because of the ever-present "white noise" from air conditioners and fluorescent lighting. The electronics of radio microphones accentuate these, resulting in a distinctive hissing or humming noise that takes away from the quality of the recording. Finding a "quiet" room can be tricky and may require you to be bold and inventive.

For example, before my interview with an economics professor in his office at Carleton University, in Ottawa, I had to lay coats and books along the top of a wheezing radiator vent to muffle the sound. On another occasion, I spent the first 10 minutes taping large manila envelopes over heating ducts in the office ceiling of a senior government executive. We had searched high and low for a "quiet" room to no avail. This comic relief actually helped us to relax with each other and produced a better interview.

Another consideration is whether you want the background sound to add to the story. Because radio works with the imagination, the background sounds, when in harmony with the content, can help the listener create mental images. If, for example, you're doing a feature on the cutthroat world of office politics, an interview with a secretary might sound more authentic over the background noise of typewriters or intercoms.

(i) The majority of interviews not done on the telephone take place where the guest works, usually at an office. Politicians and business people especially like this location, because it provides a sense of power and security and displays their status.

If you enter the lion's den with TV equipment and a crew, the balance of power in an office setting can tilt in your direction. But if you arrive with only a humble notebook or tape recorder, the trappings of power can be unsettling if you're not accustomed to them.

If you feel intimidated by your surroundings — as many people do — remember that once the person has agreed to the interview, you have a right to be there. If you can get the guest out from behind the desk, it's probably to your advantage. First of all, the desk is a physical barrier and a symbol of personal power. Second, the closer you sit to your guest, the greater the chance of intimacy and real communication. There are innumerable studies analyzing how physical distance affects relationships. You don't have to be a social scientist to know that the further away you sit from someone, the more distant your relationship. Many interviewers prefer distance, out of fear or to maintain power.

If there is a couch, suggest that it might be more comfortable to sit there. Say it's for "technical reasons," if necessary. If the guest is not willing to budge, you may have to bow to those wishes.

b. BODY POLITICS

"A person's nonverbal behavior has more bearing than words on communicating feelings or attitudes to others," says Albert Mehrabian, the author of *Silent Messages*. Mehrabian concludes that our feelings are projected to others by what we say (7%), by how we say it (38%), and by our facial expressions (55%). These figures could vary considerably depending on the culture of the speaker.

While I strongly concur that the nonverbal is of crucial importance, I believe it has to be examined in the context of what is being said. The words people use are of great significance and not to be taken lightly. There is a danger of leaning too far in the nonverbal direction and forgetting that the interviewer must deal with the total picture of what is said and how it is presented.

If the speaker's tone or body movements seem to contradict what is said, you might want to challenge the answer when it feels appropriate. But always keep in mind that this is a fallible interpretation. It is too easy to get obsessed with playing the psychological game. The nonverbal can provide great insight, but must be taken together with your intellectual response and gut feelings. Don't rely on some simplistic equation: "Aha, that scratch tells me he's lying," or "Her arms are folded, she must be defensive." Use a movement, gesture, or tone of voice to confirm your gut feeling that the person is untruthful, or that your question touched a raw nerve.

If someone says, "I don't have a problem . . . " when the tone of voice indicates the opposite, the nonverbal response overrides the verbal. In other words, rightly or wrongly, trust your gut instincts over what the person says. As long as it's considered in the context of everything that's going on, then observation of the nonverbal can be of great assistance.

1. The common touch

An experiment at an American university showed how the simple act of lightly touching someone could have a profound positive effect upon the recipient's behavior. The researchers left a coin in the return slot of a pay phone booth and watched from a vantage point as each time the coin was found and pocketed by people using the phone. Two different approaches were used by the experimenters in trying to get the coin back. In one, a researcher went over and simply asked if the person had found the coin which the researcher had "mistakenly" left behind a moment before. The coin was returned about 65% of the time. However, when the researcher gently touched the stranger before going through the identical spiel, the coin was returned about 95% of the time.

"When I have terrified guests, I touch them," says W5's Helen Hutchinson. "I sit close enough to lean over and touch them on the hand or knee. And I always keep my eyes on their eyes. I feel comfortable touching people — I do it naturally, when I'm not interviewing, so it isn't an artificial act. I would advise against people doing it as a technique, because it loses its value if it's phony."

The intent is not to turn interviewers into a pack of "touchy-feelies." Rather, it illustrates that there are ways of breaking down the natural barriers that we place between us. The action must be natural, otherwise it could make the person feel even more uncomfortable.

2. Body language cues

While nonverbal behavior can be extremely subtle, it can also be overt. I once interviewed a tall, confident-sounding director of one of the divisions of Statistics Canada in Ottawa. The interview took place, standing up, in the lobby of a government building in front of a row of unfurled provincial flags.

The subject was how bureaucrats cope with having to defend government policies they don't agree with. "I've never had that problem," said the director, brimming with sincerity. I found it difficult to believe that during 30 years as a bureaucrat the director had never disagreed with a policy. But while he continued to deny that there had ever been any conflict, he grabbed on to the edge of the flag of New Brunswick and was slowly pulling it around his body until he was literally wrapped in the flag. The scene was hilarious, for he was totally oblivious to what he'd done. I realized that no matter how smooth and at ease he sounded, the questions were striking a sensitive chord and I should persevere.

This anecdote provides a classic example of how what's really happening within us can be played out — or betrayed — by our body movements. With the caveat that these are only generalizations, here are some basic body language cues to watch for:

(a) How is the person sitting? Upright, in a comfortable assertive position? Leaning back, far away from you, per- haps with an air of indifference that suggests you're not being taken seriously? Leaning forward, moving toward you in a way that's threatening? How comfortable is the person's body? Is it rigid and unmoving in the classic "Lincoln Memorial position" — back stiff, legs apart, hands clutching the sides of the chair as if on a plane about to crash land? If so, you may have to find a way of dealing with your guest's nervousness first.

(b) Look at your guest's hands. Do they display nervousness or other emotions? Are they gripping the arms of a chair, clenched in a fist, or open and relaxed? Watch where they go during the interview. Do they go to the mouth at a certain time, trying to cover what's being spoken? Do they loosen the collar of a shirt at a crucial moment?

(c) The eyes can tell you much about what's going on inside a person. Don't get overly hung up, however, on the need for the interviewee to always look you in the eye (cultural characteristics come into play considerably). It is natural for a speaker to look away from time to time, especially if gathering thoughts. Danish psychologist Dr. Gerhard Nielsen did a study of how and where interviewees normally looked. He discovered that when people are speaking, they tend to look away; when they are listening they tend to maintain eye contact. He found that half the interviewees he observed looked away for 50% of the time. What you should assess is whether the lack of eye contact betrays anything more.

c. THE GAMES PEOPLE PLAY

Guerrilla warfare tactics are happily not the norm, but they do occur from time to time in interviews. An increasingly prominent tactic is for the interviewee to assault you with the sins of the media the minute you walk in the door. I think it's an antagonistic and foolish way for someone to begin a relationship, however brief, but when it crops up, you have to deal with it.

I let the person vent a bit of rage, using the tantrum as an opportunity to learn what I can, and then I try to put an end to it. My usual approach is to say that any profession

214

can be criticized that way, but what is more important is this specific encounter and any concerns the guest may want to raise before we start. If that doesn't work, I simply say that I don't think it's very smart to grind away at someone you're about to begin an important meeting with. If *that* doesn't work, I ask if the guest really wants to do the interview. There's only so much abuse you can endure before the power scales are tipped too heavily in the guest's direction.

There are a variety of other tricks practiced by interviewees. "My favorite trick that I've ever heard of was pulled by Salvador Dali," says Helen Hutchinson:

> He was being interviewed on film and he insisted that the interview not be run out of sequence. He didn't want it edited. He wanted to say what he had to say in the order it came out. So what he did was to wear six different brightly colored silk scarves around his neck. And at five-minute intervals he would untie one and fling it down. So, as the interview progressed, he had fewer and fewer scarves on, until the end when he had none at all. So if they cut out of sequence, the viewer could tell because the scarves would keep changing out of sequence too, which would be distracting for the viewer.

Physical appearance can also come into play. I remember a very short, senior government official who devised an ingenious way to counteract what I concluded were his feelings of physical inferiority. He had a couch and a chair in his office, an ideal setup for a radio interview. He steered me toward the chair, while he headed for the couch. When I sat in the chair, however, I disappeared into a valley of leather, with my backside almost touching the floor. Needless to say, the couch was hard as a rock and from where my guest was sitting he could now look down at me. Apart from physical discomfort, I knew I couldn't remain where I was and retain my power. Mumbling something about "technical requirements for proper miking," I got up and joined him on the couch, much to his dismay.

If you sense that your guest is uncomfortable because of differences in physical appearance, your strategy to deal with that will depend on the circumstances of the moment. The best preparation is to be aware enough to pick up on any discomfort and do what you can to alleviate it. "I'm fairly big and when I dislike someone I tend to have an aggressive edge in my voice that gives me away," says Roger Smith. "I've had to work on that, to tone it down, because it can work against me."

d. THE SEDUCTION FACTOR

It is a fascinating fact that many male interviewers describe their profession in terms of a seduction. "I find the whole interviewing process very seductive," says freelance magazine writer David Lees:

> I think [interviewing] comes naturally to people who have spent a lot of time seducing women. It's the same process. If you really want to know what a person's like inside, you have to seduce them. You've got to really drill into them, first of all to get them to tell you who they are. And you've got to be the kind of person they want to tell who they are. You have to fulfill the role so that you can be the kind of person they release themself with. And that's the essence of seduction between the sexes. The problem is that afterward, some of them feel that they've been raped.

Warner Troyer agrees with the seduction comparison, but puts the emphasis on the emotional intensity that can develop:

> Do I think it's seduction? Of course I do. Every good interviewer does it. I do it because I must. To do an interview properly I have to erase every other thing in the world. I have to concentrate totally and fully on that person. That's terribly flattering to anyone.

The seductive or flirtatious element isn't just the prerogative of male interviewers. Diane Francis of the *Toronto Star* explains how she applies it:

> I think it's a help being a female, especially in sports or business writing, because you're dealing with males and you can ask a dumb question, you can flirt and flatter and get information that way. Flirtation and flattery are two very important tools.

But to many interviewers, women in particular, the idea of using flirtation or seduction as an interviewing technique is unnecessary and offensive. "I don't see the need for it at all, for men or women," says Christina McCall:

> I don't think it's a mature way of going about doing your job. If you know what you're talking about and have any competence in speaking with people, it's a game that doesn't have to be and shouldn't be played, in my opinion.

I think there's a positive and negative side to the issue, with the key element being the intentions of the seducer. If the objective of the interviewer is to manipulate by false representation, then I equate the tactic with other deceptive and unethical practices. However, if the purpose of the interviewer is to make the guest feel special and to listen and respond with total energy, that kind of "seduction" seems to me natural and positive. Because people so infrequently experience being listened to deeply, it is very seductive to have someone focus his or her entire energy on them.

If a seduction is taking place for manipulative reasons, it may turn out to be counterproductive. Seducers are inclined to forget that it takes two to play the game. If the interviewee is going along with the seduction, what's in it for her or him?

Often it's a means of keeping the interviewer at a distance. A female friend of mine recently interviewed an attractive male who asked her to meet him in a bar. She was quite taken by his charm and looks and spent several hours taping the interview and having a few drinks. But upon returning home and listening to the tape, she realized there was little usable material. "I wasn't listening as closely as I should have been. I wasn't following up, challenging him the way I would have if I hadn't been so caught up in the sexual games between us," she told me. "I felt he was seducing me at the time, but I was enjoying it, so I didn't think about why he was doing it. My ego presumed it was just because of me."

e. THE JOY OF TAPE RECORDERS

For daily newspaper reporters or anyone working on an imminent deadline, tape-recording an interview is not practical. Not only does it take too much time to transcribe, the tendency is to have longer discussions if the tape is rolling. Most newspaper reporters prefer pencil and notebook.

I like to tape all my interviews for magazines or other long-term writing. I know my enthusiasm for the taped interview isn't universally shared, but most people's troubles with these relatively simple machines can be easily solved if a few simple procedures are followed. The fault usually lies with the user, not the machine.

1. Basic taping procedures

(a) If you buy cheap equipment, don't be surprised if it breaks down. I'm amazed at people who have the latest computer or electronic typewriter but go to tape an interview with an inexpensive, nonprofessional tape recorder. You must purchase a quality machine, one that will be dependable. Seek advice before purchasing.

(b) The most frequent technical problem you'll ever face will be battery failure. This can be eliminated if you do the following: check the batteries before leaving for the interview; have a backup set with you at all times; and have an AC cord as well. I strongly recommend you invest in a battery charger. Rechargeable batteries are less expensive by far, and you can charge them before every interview, ensuring they're at capacity power.

(c) Tape recorders are not complex machines. Take a few minutes to read the manual, and/or speak to the clerk in the store to make sure you understand how the machine works.

(d) Clean the machine occasionally. It doesn't require much maintenance, but an occasional swabbing of the recording heads with head cleaner or rubbing alcohol (unless stipulated otherwise in the manual) will help to keep it recording efficiently.

(e) Don't buy cheap cassettes. Quality recording tape, which can be reused, is not expensive. Try to have a variety of lengths of cassettes. For long, serious interviews, it's important not to have to interrupt the flow constantly to change tapes. Two-hour cassettes are excellent for this purpose.

(f) Test your tape recorder before leaving the office (or home) and then again before the actual start of the interview to make sure it's in working order. During the interview, place it in a position where you can monitor it, from time to time, to see that it's recording. At the end of each side and at the conclusion of the interview, check to see that it has recorded. Horrible as it is to discover otherwise, it's better to face that music while you're still with the guest than after you've left. If at all possible, redo the interview then and there, eliminating all unnecessary questions.

(g) Make sure you place the recorder where it can pick up both your voice and your interviewee's, especially the latter. (Miking techniques for a radio interview, as discussed in chapter 6, are different.)

(h) Be aware that the tiny microphones that come with most tape recorders are usually woefully inadequate. If you're not using the condenser (built-in) mike, make sure the freestanding mike you buy is of decent quality.

(i) If you are fearful of the machine breaking down, take notes at the same time. For magazine interviews, where you'll want to note descriptions of the interviewee and the surroundings, it's essential to use a notebook in conjunction with the tape recorder anyway.

2. Taping devices

For a few dollars you can buy a taping device that attaches, by suction cup, to the top of the outside part of the ear section of a telephone. The jack is plugged into the microphone outlet of the tape recorder. These devices, which are legal, are a godsend for doing non-broadcast telephone interviews.

They are not, however, without their pitfalls. Although the telephone line may sound fine, it's not a guarantee that the guest's voice is recording clearly. It can be extremely frustrating later trying to decipher a barely audible voice with loud static or hum interference. Because of that potential problem, monitor the interview by wearing an earphone as you're doing the interview, and/or take notes as you go along. The earphones will give you a more accurate idea of how the guest's voice is being reproduced, so you can call back to try and get a clearer line, or take notes, before it's too late.

There is no legal obligation in Canada to inform someone if you are taping the conversation, just as you don't have to divulge that you're taking notes. What you do with the tape is another matter. It can't be broadcast without the interviewee's consent, a permission that it would be wise to have on tape.

In the United States, although legislation varies from state to state, it's wise to get permission both to tape the interview and to broadcast it. If in doubt, check with your local state authorities.

3. Benefits of taping interviews

(a) It provides 100% accuracy. Handwritten notes are often inaccurate or incomplete.

(b) It gives a record of the speaker's voice, which can reveal meaning, attitude, emotion, etc. Cold scribbles, looked at some time after the interview, do not.

(c) It provides proof that the quotes are accurate. This protects you, more than notes will, if an interviewee threatens legal action or cries misquote. Many publications insist you tape interviews for those reasons.

(d) Many interviewees, especially in industry and government, bring *their* tape recorders to an interview. It is not a good situation for an interviewee to have a verbatim record while you only have partial notes.

(e) A tape recorder frees you to listen attentively, observe nonverbal behavior, and work at establishing rapport with the guest.

f. THE CASE FOR TAKING NOTES

Interviewers who prefer note taking cite speed and concentration as the primary reasons for their preference other than their distrust of things mechanical.

"There usually isn't enough time to transcribe interviews for daily journalism," says Judy Nyman of the *Toronto Star*:

> I find people are more intimidated by tape recorders than by notebooks. I'll only tape if there's a possibility of some legal action or if it's a personality profile or feature where I want to get really meaty, complete quotes. I never learned shorthand. I highly recommend that anyone who wants to be a reporter should. I've developed my own shorthand style over the years, that only I can read, and I have to write up my notes within a couple of days or even I don't know what they mean.

To avoid that problem, Wade Rowland, who was a newspaperman before moving over to broadcasting, says, "You should go over and enlarge upon your notes as soon as you can after the interview. I like to sit down with a coffee and work on them right away."

There are also psychological ploys involved in note taking, as Richard Gwyn explains:

Note taking has a double function. One is simply to take notes. The other is to encourage the person to open up. Sometimes I'll take notes on something I'll never use. It's a way of saying, come on, you're doing okay. I'm trying to signal the person. If you don't take notes they get kind of upset. Sometimes, by deliberately not taking notes, you can goad them into saying more. It's a way of signalling that you don't think they're saying anything of value.

A notebook can make it easier for people to suspend their disbelief and imagine that what they're saying isn't really being officially noted. With tape recorders, interviewees know they can't blame the reporter for having misquoted them.

Taking notes also helps remind you to get the correct spellings, ascertain titles, and check other essential details as you go along. It's easy to overlook that function when you're taping an interview, an omission that can cost you later on when you're writing the story and might not be able to get in touch with the source.

g. OFF-THE-RECORD

The thorny question of off-the-record is constantly debated, with no clear-cut principles across the board. Charles Lynch of Southam News says, "We are in the business of disclosing and everything is on-the-record." Arch MacKenzie of Canadian Press says: "Off-the-record is off-the-record."

Since there are clearly no consistent guidelines, it's important to have your own policy. In formulating it, here are some points to consider:

(a) Many people tell you something is off-the-record when the information is readily available on-the-record. Wade Rowland says:

When I'm told something is going to be off-the-record, there's an immediate and serious question in my mind as to whether I want to know it from that guy or whether I want to find it out from someone else. Generally speaking, in 99% of the cases, what they're telling you off-the-record you can get on-the-record from someone else and you're not bound by the restrictions that way.

(b) Off-the-record is a valuable way of getting information that you need to know, even if you can't quote it. People in sensitive positions may not want to be quoted for fear of losing their jobs, but may want to help you. This should be weighed before you decide whether to agree to a privileged conversation (i.e., off-the-record).

(c) Can the information be attributed to an unidentified source? This practice, known as NFA (not for attribution) should not be used unless necessary, since getting attributable quotes is vital to fair journalism. Be careful not to give the person's identity away by careless description — for example, mentioning a "senior official in the minister's office," when there could only be one senior official who knows the information quoted.

(d) Above all else, I think you must have a sensitivity for the people you interview. What effect will the information have on the personal life and livelihood of your source if the quotes are attributed? Author William Manchester cautions interviewers to be especially careful with people who are inexperienced interviewees. "They forget it's an interview and they let all sorts of personal details spill out," he says. "Then it becomes an invasion of privacy, which is something that one must be careful of."

h. SUBMITTING QUESTIONS

Some interviewees request advance submission of questions. This practice usually results in people preparing formal, usually cautious, answers, and the interview becomes a recitation rather than a natural dialogue. If you are restricted to asking only the prearranged questions, you don't get a chance to ask follow-ups, which are usually the meat of the interview. A compromise might be to offer the guest a list of areas you wish to cover, which often satisfies his or her need for some advance notice of what to expect.

However, if there's no other way to get the interview, then what do you have to lose? "I don't like to submit questions but I figure that once you're in there, you're in there and anything can happen," says Roy MacGregor, implying that once you get your toe in the door, there's a chance for a real interview to take place.

Other interviewees will demand approval of the story before it can go to print. In almost all cases, I've found the interviewee will back down if you stick to your guns and explain why you won't acquiesce. The reasons you can offer are straightforward. First, a newspaper, magazine, or broadcast outlet must have control of its own product. Second, interviewees are not professional journalists and may demand the removal of some information that is absolutely essential to the story. Third, people tend to be ultra-sensitive about how they are described, or how they appear in print or sound on tape. If they're allowed to vet copy, they tend to soften it, an unacceptable condition for a publisher or producer.

However, there can be situations where collaboration is beneficial. If you're working on a highly technical, complicated story, it can be lifesaving to have one of your contacts look over the copy for accuracy. Or whenever you're in doubt about some material, it's usually helpful to phone one or more of the interviewees and read particular sections to them. I've found that I've caught many errors by doing that.

i. CONCLUSION

Although this book contains much information about the techniques and methods of interviewing, I want to emphasize more than anything else that interviewing is an individual experience, one that involves far more than knowing a set of rules or mastering the tricks of the trade.

The techniques presented are only guidelines to be adapted to each person's particular needs and style.

Interviewing is essentially about interpersonal relationships, and how we communicate with each other. While I understood that point on a certain level before I began work on the book, I came to understand it much more deeply through the intensive process of researching, speaking with many interviewers and interviewees, and putting my thoughts about interviewing down on paper. I believe our development as interviewers is intricately linked to our development as individuals: the more we know about ourselves and other people, the more we know about how to speak and relate to them. The potential for personal growth and development, through stimulating conversations with fascinating people, is boundless.

FEATURE INTERVIEW: Patrick Watson

Patrick Watson was exhausted at the end of our two-hour interview. And understandably so, for he had expended what seemed like his total energy into our conversation. While some people sit and politely answer questions, Watson put on a performance, telling anecdotes with dramatic flair, lowering and raising his voice for effect, mimicking accents, doing whatever was needed to amplify what he was saying and hold my attention. As I felt the thrust of his concentration and interest, I understood what made him such a successful interviewer.

Watson's resume is far too long to reproduce. Suffice to say that he is the preeminent male TV interviewer in Canada, an accomplished author and versatile actor. We had met for lunch prior to the interview, Watson's suggestion. Before sitting down for a formal session, he wanted to get a sense of who I was, for we had never met before. Following a long lunch, we walked to his home and did the interview:

PM: Where did you learn to interview?

PW: The first interviews I did were on television. They were on a children's program called *Junior Magazine*, in the mid-1950s . . . oriented toward 8- to 14-year-olds. And somehow early on I caught the notion, I think, that one of the most important objectives was the person and not the subject . . . — that what we are doing for an audience is revealing a person. If it happens that this person is an expert in railway timetables, in the course of the interview we may find ourselves becoming interested in railway timetables. And I might, at that point, have even thought we would learn something about railway timetables. I now know better. The only thing that you learn from a television interview is that railway timetables are either interesting or not interesting. But you may learn that there are people in the world who are absolutely bloody spellbound at how you put a railway timetable together, and that in itself, and the exposure to that person, is a valuable kind of communication.

Now, in the period between that time and the time I began to work as a contract producer for what was then called public affairs [a department at CBC] I think I sort of forgot some of that. I was exposed to a lot of quite scholarly people in the department, most of whom had come from radio, to whom the subject under discussion was paramount. And so for a while I was pretty frustrated to find that a lot of programs on which we sweated and I thought were damn good, well-organized programs, had first, not reached very big audiences and, second, the audience reached were often indifferent, often not very lucid about what had been discussed and, third, and most provocative, had liked the program best when there was a lot of shouting and yelling but not too much discussion. That began by frustrating me, and then reflections on that led me to retrieve some of the earlier nature of the television interview and get back to the idea that the experience of meeting people was what counted.

PM: Wouldn't people's reaction be, "Surely if you have a cabinet minister on and you're talking about a new, controversial piece of legislation, that the legislation is more important than the person?"

PW: Well, in that case, why not read the legislation? It seems to me that, of course, there is a *de facto* truth about that kind of comment. You have to know what the legislation is and your questions have to be pertinent and correct. What is important on television, though, is the public witness, to use the good 'ole Christian term, that has taken place. In which you, as a steward of the public interest on one side, or out of one matrix, and the cabinet minister, as a steward of the public interest out of another matrix, are acting out responsibilities in front of the public in a theatrical forum. And those people who know something about the legislation will remember some of what is said. Almost nobody else will. But what will be seen is the way in which the two participants fulfill their stewardship and responsibilities to the public. And that's important. That's the unique thing that the television interview does that no other one does. Radio comes close. But television, because one sees expression, one reads body language and so on, deals with the reactions of persons, not just with the conveying of ideas.

PM: How strong do you think the non-verbal message that the guest gives is in relation to the verbal?

PW: Normally when you say non-verbal you're thinking body language, facial expression, what the eyes do, and all that kind of stuff which is critical, vital. But to distinguish from print, certainly, the aspects of voice quality which are not verbal, in the sense that they are not translated by a transcript, are equally important.

PM: How reliable do you think that information is?

PW: The very best you can say to yourself is that there are occasionally moments that happen in the spontaneous television interview in which you just know, with all your profound intuition, that there is some kind of truth taking place here, some kind of revelation. Even then, sometimes you're wrong. . . . The umbrella statement is that in a universe saturated with different kinds of information, as ours is, television is one component that can be cross-checked against a lot of others. And one should virtually never accept one component of that information universe as being "the" answer to that person.

PM: This may seem too obvious, but how much do you pay attention during an interview?

PW: Somewhere along the line I learned that that's the most important thing you can do, is to pay attention. And to make a very careful plan and do a lot of research and then effectively throw the plan away.

PM: Have it as a back-up?

PW: Well, it's rather more. Assuming that if the plan was any good in the first place, you're going to remember the essentials of it and the things that you're going to forget, on the whole, are better off forgotten. This is a lesson I learned from Bucky Fuller, with whom I spent a lot of time exploring issues of spontaneity and the capacity of the human brain to do the right thing at the right time if you give it a chance. At some point I decided, in almost a doctrinaire or superstitious way, that the interview was almost certainly going to be better if I did not even take the physical notes into the studio. And so I stopped doing that.

PM: But you weren't going in cold, though. I presume you'd go in with objectives.

PW: Oh, [I'd go] in with a lot of objectives, often carefully worked out route maps, traps. . . .

PM: Would you role-play a difficult interview in your mind?

PW: Sometimes not only in my mind, often I'd do it with Leiterman (Doug Leiterman, producer and sometime interviewer on *This Hour Has Seven Days*, among other credits). Sometimes switching. He'd be me and I'd be the guest.

PM: I try to get my students to do this but —

PW: They think it's silly. You've got to convince them that the television interview, if it is nothing else, has got to be theater or it won't work. So they might as well rehearse.

PM: So what does that make the interviewer?

PW: Well, he's both an actor and a director. He's producing and directing this theatrical event while he's doing it, in collaboration with [many] others.

PM: Are you aware of your own body language, of the use of your own voice?

PW: Yes, I am. I'm not sure what to recommend to people about that. I think partly because of my interest and time in theater, I'm not uncomfortable about being an actor. And I think it may be very tough to ask everybody to be an actor, to the extent that I'm prepared to do, which involves looking at yourself with considerable care. I believe it helps a great deal to be fairly deliberate about it. And here's the great contradiction. You're both deliberate about it, but you're also prepared to be spontaneous, prepared to let stuff happen and forget about it.

PM: And they can co-exist?

PW: They can. I did an interview with Pinchas Zukerman on a *Live From Lincoln Center* concert last week. And he talked about a similar level of consciousness that he finds himself in when he's playing. I saw Zukerman backstage, he was amiable, joking with the technicians and the conductor. But then on stage, instrument to the chin [violin], he gets the bow up there and a mask comes down and the face goes deadpan, immobile, and the body doesn't move very much. So I was asking about that. Was that a discipline, a trick? And he began to talk in a way that was absolutely germane to what we're talking about. About the multiple levels of consciousness that are working while he's playing. One is dealing exclusively with the music as music that he is hearing. Another is dealing with the audience hearing the music. And who is this audience and what's the size of the hall? Another is dreaming something that has nothing to do with any of this. Another is watching himself. . . . You're observing the event from a number of different points of view.

PM: Do you find a difference between interviewing men and women?

PW: Yes, but I would be very hard-pressed to analyze it for you. . . .

PM: What are your views on the confrontational interview these days?

PW: I think there's a place for it . . . but in a sense the confrontational interview is a less mature form than the one in which you are really interested, more than anything else, in revealing the person. And revealing the person may include some elements of confrontation, but it really requires a discipline on the part of the interviewer that says, the primary purpose to be served here is to strip away. Not to win in an exchange, but to strip away so that people will feel that the room has disappeared and the set has disappeared and they are in the presence of the person. So that requires you to have at your disposal a lot of mechanisms besides knowing a lot of intimate details about the subject's life. It requires you to have compassion, to be prepared to empathize, prepared to listen and understand.

PM: What if you are beating someone up. Do you believe that the smart interviewer backs off?

PW: Depends on what you want to do. If you want to protect yourself, you better back off. But if your objective is to demonstrate to the audience that this person — say someone who is after public office — can't stand up to continual harassment and yet is asking for your vote, then maybe you are serving the audience best if you accept the fact that they are going to hate you, but you better keep on going after him.

PM: A lot of people talk about interviews in terms of winning or losing.

PW: That's unfortunate, but it's an inevitable criterion when you've got a confrontational interview. You cannot see other than in terms of a prize fight. The interviewer who is interested in making something happen with the audience has to say to himself, what's more important? That I win in those terms or that the audience wins? So you gotta be prepared to lose.

[At this point, I sensed his energy was fading. "Anything you'd like to say that I haven't asked you?" I asked. "No, I'm getting tired," he replied. "If you want a follow-up, you could come back." The next morning, however, it was Watson who wanted to follow-up. He telephoned, concerned that he had placed too much emphasis on the theater of the interview and not acknowledged enough the value of the content.]

PW: I just wanted to speak further about the seeming insistence of mine that nobody remembers what is said [in a TV interview]. That changes radically as soon as people start telling stories; or, in the interview situation, as soon as you have a very clear, dramatic conflict going on between two people around an issue that's very prominent. That kind of talk will be remembered. I remember interviewing Joe Clark during an election campaign when he was the leader. There was a moment in which he had presented himself, in a very tight, concrete statement, as, in fact, knowing better than the people of Canada. And it was so anti-democratic that just confronting him with that issue turned out to be a memorable moment because he obviously could not back it up. And that little moment was the kind of thing that sticks in the mind and people remember the words of it.

PM: However, I still agree that the impression is what results more than anything else from, say, a half hour interview. A week later you might not remember much of what he said, but you will remember how you felt about him.

PW: Oh yes. I'm not contradicting that and that's absolutely the overrriding consideration. It's just that I didn't want to leave the impression that I thought nobody remembered anything that was said.

The second thing I wanted to mention is that the broadcast interview is a very sweet opportunity to contradict the conventional wisdom or the popular illusory mythology about a person or about an issue that the person is involved in. . . . To attack the popular wisdom is something that seems to work in the interview format. And I think it is extremely important, when preparing an interview, that the interviewer take a look at his subject and try to identify the principal categories of mythology around this person. This person is thought to be a great lover, or the principal advocate of radical right wing extremism when it comes to capital punishment. . . . And ask, what are the opposites? What is it in the background of the person that may be contradictory to that? In every personality, it seems to me there is always a set of opposites at work. The person who is a devout advocate of censorship has somewhere in his personal makeup a profound libidinous prurience.

Some of the best writing about that particular aspect of the personality, both on the individual level and the social level, is a wonderful book called *The Pursuit of Loneliness*, by Philip Slater. It's a fabulous analysis of the American social personality, which starts out as a kind of paradigm of a number of national characteristics — the Germans, the British, etc. — in terms of those kinds of opposites.

PM: I find that, especially in interviews that aren't done properly or are under a tight deadline, the easiest thing to do is to reinforce the mythology, the stereotype.

PW: Absolutely. And, in fact, the interview subject will cheerfully go along with that because it's lazy and it's easy. Even if he's not necessarily committed to the maintaining of that mythology and would probably welcome and find refreshing a detour out of that kind of iconic prison. He's not likely to do it without being provoked. And once he's provoked, it could be very interesting.

PM: How strongly do you study the human psyche? How much store do you put in understanding psychology?

PW: I've done a lot of reading in the field, psychological literature, and I think it's important to be thinking about the kinds of analyses that the great writers in the field have made. Rollo May, for example, has a book called *Power and Innocence*, the thesis of which is that violence emerges among the powerless; and the truly powerful persons are those you can really count on for gentleness and sensitivity. That it is disempowerment that generates violent behavior. That sounds like a kind of banal thing, but that little insight I have found very useful in dealing with people who have behaved erratically. Just asking myself, what happened to this person who seems in control of his life, who has the trappings of power, and has suddenly burst out and done something erratic. There must have been a disempowerment that led to that.

THE BUSINESS GUIDE TO EFFECTIVE SPEAKING
Making presentations, using audio-visuals, and dealing with the media

Give dynamic speeches, presentations, and media interviews. When you are called upon to speak in front of your business colleagues, or asked to represent your company in front of the media, do you communicate your thoughts effectively? Or do you become tongue-tied, nervous, and worry about misrepresenting yourself and your business?

Effective communication has always been the key to business success, and this book provides a straightforward approach to developing techniques to improve your on-the-job speaking skills. This book is as easy to pick up and use as a quick reference for a specific problem as it is to read from cover to cover. Whether you want to know how to deal with the media, when to use visual aids in a presentation, or how to prepare for chairing a meeting, this book will answer your questions and help you regain your confidence. $7.95

Contents include:

- Preparing your presentation
- When and where will you speak?
- Let's look at visual aids
- Let's hear what you have to say: rehearsing
- How do you sound?
- What is your body saying about you?
- Confidence and self-control
- Packaging the presenter

RADIO DOCUMENTARY HANDBOOK
Creating, producing, and selling for broadcast

This book is about writing, producing and selling a radio documentary. You've got a great idea for a radio documentary, but how do you get it on the air? Who do you talk to? How do you put it together? Is the radio documentary a product of creative genius? Or can you acquire skills that will guarantee good results every time?

This guide is an invaluable tool for broadcast journalists, students of journalism and communications, public relations professionals, and anyone else whose work involves taping for radio. $8.95

Contents include:

- The idea's the thing

- Choosing a format

- Making a proposal

- Getting organized

- Doing the research

- Finding people to interview

- Selecting your recording hardware

- Using a microphone

- Recording sound effects and music

- Dubbing recorded material

- Reviewing your components

- How to pick, save, and discard

- The secret of editing

PRACTICAL TIME MANAGEMENT
How to get more things done in less time

Are you always short of time? Here is sound advice
for anyone who needs to develop practical time
management skills. It is designed to help any busy
person, from any walk of life, use his or her time
more effectively. Not only does it explain how to easily get more things done, it shows you how your self-
esteem will improve in doing so. More important,
emphasis is placed on maintenance so that you
remain in control. Whether you want to find extra
time to spend with your family or to read the latest
bestseller, this book will give you the guidance you
need — without taking up a lot of your time! $6.95

Contents include:

- Getting more things done

- Decide what you want to do

- How do you spend your time?

- Overcoming inertia

- Planning to finish

- Managing leisure time

- The new you

LEARN TO TYPE FAST
Completely new, easy method for beginners

A fast new method for learning to type fast. This book takes the mystique out of learning to type. The author, after years of teaching typing, has devised a unique method for learning to type that eliminates the frustration and tedium found in most how-to-type books.

By using this new system, you can learn to type in five hours! Short review sessions serve to reinforce the basic skills learned in ten half-hour lessons. The system is based on learning the typewriter keys in relation to your fingers, rather than the typewriter keyboard. This means you can learn the keys quickly and automatically even if you aren't at the typewriter! $11.95

Contents include:

- How to use the finger labeling method
- Ten wall charts to use for each lesson
- The four common characteristics of good typists
- How to measure your progress
- How to do tabulations and number typing
- How to do centering and set up letter styles
- What you need to know about word processing typing
- How to increase your speed once you know how to type

BUSINESS ETIQUETTE TODAY
A guide to corporate success

Mind your manners and get ahead! Knowing when to open the door for a colleague or how to accept a gift can sometimes mean the difference between being pigeon-holed in your current position or being offered that attractive promotion. But times have also changed, and the rules once relied on are not always appropriate today. With the growing number of women in company boardrooms and the move toward more international business, a new style of behavior is often called for.

This book is as easy to pick up and use as a quick reference before that special event as it is to read cover to cover. $7.95

Contents include:

- To begin at the beginning — the etiquette of employment
- Department decorum
- Telephone manners
- Meeting manners and boardroom behavior
- Introductions and conversation
- Cultural courtesy
- Table manners
- Eating in and dining out
- Giving and receiving — the etiquette of business gifts
- Put it in writing
- Manners on the road

ORDERING INFORMATION

All prices are subject to change without notice. Books are available in book, department, and stationery stores, or use this order form. (Please print)

IN CANADA
Please send your order to the nearest location:
Self-Counsel Press, 1481 Charlotte Road,
North Vancouver, B. C. V7J 1H1
Self-Counsel Press, #8-2283 Argentia Road,
Mississauga, Ontario L5N 5Z2

IN THE U.S.A.
Please send your order to:
Self-Counsel Press Inc., 1704 N. State Street, Bellingham, WA 98225

Name _____

Address _____

_____

Charge to:
❏Visa   ❏ MasterCard

Account Number _____

Validation Date_____

Expiry Date _____

Signature _____

❏Check here for a free catalogue.

Please add $2.50 for postage & handling.
WA residents please add 7.8% sales tax

In Canada, please add 7% GST to all orders.

YES, please send me
_____copies of **The Business Guide to Effective Speaking**, $7.95
_____copies of **Radio Documentary Handbook**, $8.95
_____copies of **Practical Time Management**, $6.95
_____copies of **Learn to Type Fast**, $11.95
_____copies of **Business Etiquette Today**, $7.95